W9-ADW-488

THE ART OF AUDUBON

THE ART OF AUDUBON

The Complete Birds and Mammals

JOHN JAMES AUDUBON

With an Introduction by Roger Tory Peterson

Second printing, August 1980

Published by TIMES BOOKS, a division
of Quadrangle/The New York Times Book Co., Inc.
Three Park Avenue, New York, N.Y. 10016

Published simultaneously in Canada by
Fitzhenry & Whiteside, Ltd., Toronto.

Library of Congress Cataloging in Publication Data

Audubon, John James, 1785–1851.
The art of Audubon.

Includes index.
1. Birds—North America—Pictorial works.
2. Mammals—North America—Pictorial works.
I. Title.
QL681.A96 1979 599'.09'70222 79-51434
ISBN 0-8129-0841-4

Manufactured in the United States of America.

Contents

BIRDS BY FAMILY

MAMMALS BY GENUS

Introduction

Although John James Audubon was an emigre from France when he came to the United States at the age of eighteen, he was actually born in the West Indies in the year 1785. His mother was a genteel French-Creole lady and his father a prosperous French sea-captain, who after reverses in Les Cayes in Santo Domingo, now Haiti, where he owned an estate, returned to France. There the youthful Jean Jacques Fougere Audubon received a young gentleman's tutoring and even studied drawing under the guidance of the master, Jacques Louis David.

Audubon's odyssey in North America has been recounted many times; how his father sent him to his farm at Mill Grove near Philadelphia, and later set him up in business in Kentucky where he met with successive business failures as he moved westward to the Mississippi and then down to New Orleans. There his devoted wife, Lucy, supported herself and their two sons while her wandering husband was away many months at a time exploring the wilderness, painting, and prodigiously pursuing his dream of producing the epic work on the birds of North America.

Elemental forces were at work within Audubon—the stuff of which artists, poets and prophets are made. Birds were the hub around which his world revolved; their furious pace of living, their beauty, their mystery, reflected the subtle forces that guided his own life.

He was unworldly, yet closely attuned to the natural world. His simplicity, tremendous vitality, enthusiasm for life in all its variety, and his drive for creative excellence made him one of the most enduring personalities in American history.

Audubon's portraits of birds, the product of more than thirty years of field work and labor at the drawing board, were engraved by Robert Havell, Jr. of London who undertook the herculean eleven-year task of reproduction and even introduced minor changes of his own into some of the compositions and backgrounds. They were published as "The Birds of America" in four huge volumes (the largest weighing 56 pounds) between the years of 1827 and 1838. In his 435 color plates, Audubon depicted the birds exactly the size of life. Even the oversize format, known as "double elephant folio," the largest ever attempted in the history of book publishing, was insufficient to accommodate the large birds comfortably, with the result that tall birds such as the flamingo and the great blue heron are shown with their long necks drooped toward their feet. On the other hand, tiny birds like kinglets and hummingbirds are all but lost on the page.

Although Audubon's immortality rests largely on his work as an artist, he was no less of an ornithologist. The extraordinary amount of observation detailed in his five-volume, three thousand-page *Ornithological Biography,* edited and rewritten in part by William MacGillivray and published almost concurrently with his *Birds of America* between the years of 1831 and 1839 as a supplemental descriptive text relating to the plates, remains as the baseline for comparing the status of birds then and now. No less important as an historical record are the comments they contain on places, people and customs.

Later, Audubon prepared a seven-volume octavo edition of his *Birds of America,* adding 65 more color plates and incorporating the text from his *Ornithological Biography.* This first octavo edition was published in New York and Philadelphia between the years of 1840 and 1844.

In reviewing Audubon's massive tour-de-force, his paintings seem to fall into at least three categories. We usually think of Audubon's style as patternistic or decorative on an open white background. Actually, the leaves, flowers and other accessories were often painted in by apprentice artists, notably Joseph Mason and George Lehman. At a later period he produced many bird portraits with solid environmental backgrounds, usually southern scenes, which were executed largely by Lehman. Among the last few plates and the 65 additional ones included in the later octavo edition are birds from the western part of the country. These are perhaps his least successful efforts. He may have grown tired of his seemingly endless projects, but a fairer judgment is that he had seen few of these birds in life. They are drawn from specimens sent to him by Nuttall, Swainson, Townsend, and Gould.

It was inevitable that after he had painted and described all the birds then known from North America, Audubon would apply his brush and pen to the mammals with which he also had a lifelong intimacy.

In the Harvard University Library there is a crayon sketch of a marmot dashed off by Audubon when he revisited France at the age of twenty. It is believed to be his earliest drawing of a mammal. Even when he was deeply involved with his bird portraiture he occasionally found time to draw mammals. A recurrent theme was an otter in a trap, which he painted again and again both in watercolor and in oils, particularly when he was in need of funds. A particularly skilled version was hung in an exhibition at the Scottish Academy.

Actually, Audubon conceived the idea of a comparable mammal publication several years earlier during conversations with the Reverend John Bachman of South Carolina, himself a naturalist of considerable scholarship, who warned Audubon of the technical problems they faced. He emphasized that mammals, because of their more secretive habits, would be more difficult to paint and to write about than birds. It was agreed that Bachman would act as co-author and editor of the three biographical volumes which were to accompany the three-volume folio of mammal portraits. The whole enterprise was impressively titled *The Viviparous Quadrupeds of North America.*

Audubon's two grown sons, John and Victor, had become full-fledged assistants in the production of his *Birds of America* by 1836. Both were learning to paint creditably, and John Woodhouse Audubon in particular gave promise of a talent that could equal his father's. The two boys married the two elder daughters of the Reverend Bachman, a family merger that was to end tragically when John's wife Maria, then 23, died of tuberculosis, leaving two small children. She was followed in death less than a year later by Victor's wife, Mary Eliza, plunging Audubon into the greatest grief he had known since the death of his own two infant daughters.

Bachman felt it was very important that Audubon, then in his late fifties, should go west to investigate some of the mammals of the frontier. His trip in 1843 to the headwaters of the Missouri and the mouth of the Yellowstone was his last great field expedition. After risking death at the hands of Sioux and Assiniboines and other adventures, he returned to his New York City estate, Minniesland, where he devoted his waning energies to the *Quadrupeds* which were to be published by J. T. Bowen of Philadelphia. His eyes and his mind were no longer equal to the strain, so in 1846 he began to rely more on his two talented sons. He had already painted more than 100 of the 150 colorplates. His son John painted the rest under close supervision while Victor skillfully put in the backgrounds. The remainder of the biographies were entirely the work of Reverend Bachman.

Audubon did not live to see the *Quadrupeds* completed. He died in 1851 at the age of 66.

Audubon might rightly have been called the "Father of American Ornithology" had not the Scot, Alexander Wilson, preceded him by about twenty years in the publication of his own *American Ornithology.* Although Wilson was able to find a publisher in the United States, Audubon had to go to England to find backers and printers for his larger, more ambitious folio of paintings. A total of about 190 sets were eventually bound and distributed. Less than half exist today; the others were acquired by dealers who broke them up and sold the prints individually.

Twelve years after Audubon's death, his widow sold his original paintings to the New York Historical Society where they can be seen to this day, forever safeguarded.

Audubon was the epitome of the hunter-naturalist. Modern critics sometimes point out that as a young man he found too much delight in shooting birds; he was "in blood up to his elbows." This is abundantly borne out by his *Ornithological Biography* in which he details the number of specimens he took, often far more than he needed for his portraits or his anatomical studies.

It would therefore seem inappropriate that the foremost conservation organization in the United States should adopt his name, but not so. Actually, Audubon was ahead of his time. Like so many thoughtful sportsmen since, he eventually developed a conservation conscience. In an era when there were no game laws, no national parks or refuges, when vulnerable nature gave way to human pressures and often sheer stupidity, when there was no environmental ethic, he was a witness who sounded the alarm. He became more and more concerned during his later travels when, with the perspective of his years, he could see the trend. He wrote vividly and passionately about what he saw and some of the passages in his writings were very prophetic.

Today Audubon, who wished to be known primarily as an artist, is considered the patron saint of American wildlife conservation. His name, long synonymous with birds, has become a symbol of our need to understand the environment and to live in harmony with all that is natural.

And as long as our civilization lasts, America will be in debt to this genius.

Roger Tory Peterson

PUBLISHER'S NOTE

One of the last major publishing projects on which John James Audubon embarked was the complete Octavo edition of his paintings. Containing 500 engravings of birds, partially revised from the original "double elephant folio" edition, the Octavo edition was finally published in seven volumes in the 1840s. Until now, the Octavo edition of Audubon's birds together with his 150 engravings of *Quadrupeds* have never been assembled and published in a single volume.

The bird and mammal sections have been separately arranged in a logical pattern to provide clear comparison within each individual species. Following a scientific order originally devised by Audubon, the publisher has divided the bird engravings by family and sub-divided them by genus. With each individual genus, the birds have been alphabetically positioned according to the first name on the engraving. The mammals have been grouped by Latin genus name, and the genus names have subsequently been alphabetized.

Over the years many changes have been made in Audubon's scientific names. For example, *Bison Americanus* is now *Bison Bison; Ursa Ferox* is now *Ursa Horribilis.* Also, Audubon divided the cats into two classifications *(Felis* and *Lynx),* a distinction that is no longer in use. There are undoubtedly many other changes which have come about in scientific nomenclature since the 1840s, but this new edition is as close to Audubon's original designations as is possible.

At the end of the volume, two indices have been provided, separately listing the birds and mammals within an English-Latin and Latin-English context.

BOOK OF BIRDS

No. 1

Pl. 1

Californian Turkey Vulture

Drawn from Nature by J. J. Audubon, F.R.S.F.L.S.

Lithd. printed & Cold. by J. T. Bowen, Phila.

No. 1

Pl. 3

Black Vulture or Carrion Crow.

Drawn from Nature by J.J. Audubon, F.R.S.F.L.S.

Lith.d printed & Col.d by J.T. Bowen, Phila.

Red-headed Turkey Vulture.

Drawn from Nature by J. J. Audubon, F.R.S.F.L.S. Lith.d printed & Col.d by J. T. Bowen, Phil.a

No. 1 Pl. 4

Caracara Eagle

Drawn from Nature by J. J. Audubon, F.R.S. F.L.S. Lithd. printed & Cold. by J. T. Bowen, Philda.

Broad-winged Buzzard.

Drawn from Nature by J.J.Audubon. F.R.S.F.L.S.

Lithd. Printed & Cold. by J.T. Bowen. Philada.

N°2

Pl. 6

Common Buzzard.

COMMON BUZZARD.

Drawn from Nature by J.J.Audubon.F.R S.F.L.S.

No. 2

Pl. 8.

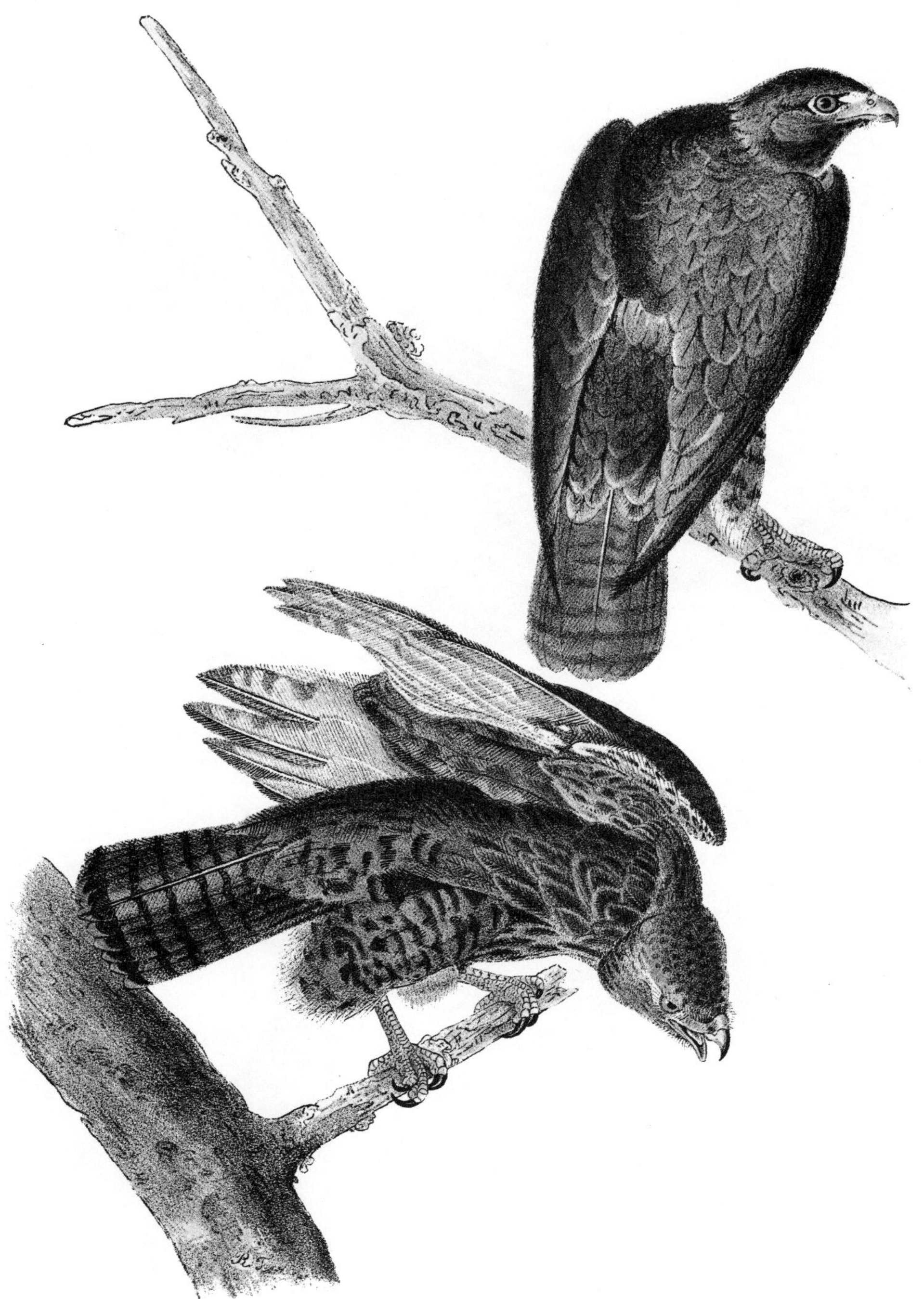

Harlan's Buzzard.

Drawn from Nature by J.J. Audubon, F.R.S.F.L.S.

Lith.d Printed & Col.d by J. T. Bowen, Philad.a

No. 1 Pl 5

Harris's Buzzard

Drawn from Nature by J. J. Audubon, F.R.S.F.L.S.   Lith. printed & Col. by J. T. Bowen, Phila.

Red-shouldered Buzzard

Drawn from Nature by J.J. Audubon, F.R.S.F.L.S. Lith.d Printed & Col.d by J. T. Bowen, Philad.a

No. 2. Pl. 7.

Red-tailed Buzzard.

Drawn from Nature by J.J. Audubon, F.R.S.F.L.S.

Lith.d Printed & Col.d by J. T. Bowen, Philad.a

No. 3. Pl. 11.

R.F.

Rough-legged Buzzard.

Drawn from nature by J.J.Audubon F.R.S.F.L.S.

Lith^d. Printed & Col^d. by J.T. Bowen, Philad^a.

No. 3. Pl. 12.

Golden Eagle.

Drawn from Nature by J.J. Audubon, F.R.S.F.L.S. Lith.d Printed & Col.d by J. T. Bowen, Philad.a

N°3

Pl. 10.

Washington Sea Eagle.

Drawn from Nature by J. J. Audubon F.R.S. F.L.S.

Lith.d Printed & Col.d by J. T. Bowen Philad.a

N° 3. Pl. 14.

White-headed Sea Eagle, or Bald Eagle.

Drawn from Nature by J.J.Audubon, F.R.S.F.L.S.

Lith.d Printed & Col.d by J.T. Bowen, Philad.a

Nº 3

Pl. 15.

Common Osprey. Fish Hawk.

Drawn from Nature by J. J. Audubon. F.R.S.F.L.S.

Lith.d Printed & Col.d by J. T. Bowen. Philad.a

Black-shouldered Elanus.

Drawn from Nature by J.J.Audubon. F.R.S.F.L.S. Lith.d Printed & Col.d by J.T.Bowen. Philad.a

Mississipi Kite.

Drawn from Nature by J. J. Audubon. F.R.S.F.L.S. Lithd Printed & Cold by J. T. Bowen. Philada

N° 4

Pl. 18

Swallow-tailed Hawk.

Drawn from Nature by J. J. Audubon F.R.S. F.L.S.

Lith.d Printed & Col.d by J.T. Bowen, Philad.a

R.T.

Iceland or Gyr Falcon.

Drawn from Nature by J.J.Audubon.F.R.S.F.L.S.

Lith^d Printed & Col^d by J.T.Bowen, Philad^a

No. 4

Pl. 20

Peregrine Falcon.

Drawn from Nature by J. J. Audubon. F.R.S. F.L.S.

Lith.d Printed & Col.d by J. T. Bowen, Philad.a

N° 5 Pl. 21

Pigeon Falcon.

Drawn from Nature by J. J. Audubon F.R.S.F.L.S. Lith.d Printed & Col.d by J. T. Bowen Philad.

No. 5 PL. 22.

Sparrow Falcon.

Drawn from Nature by J. J. Audubon. F.R.S.F.L.S. Lith.d Printed & Col.d by J. T. Bowen, Philad.a

No. 5 Pl. 23.

Goshawk.

Drawn from Nature by J. J. Audubon, F.R.S.F.L.S.

Lith.d Printed & Col.d by J. T. Bowen Philada.

Cooper's Hawk.

Drawn from Nature by J. J. Audubon F.R.S.F.L.S. Lith^d Printed & Col^d by J.T. Bowen, Philad^a.

No. 5

Pl. 25

R. T.

Sharp-shinned Hawk.

Drawn from Nature by J. J. Audubon. F.R.S.F.L.S.

Lith.d Printed & Col.d by J. T. Bowen. Philad.a

No. 6. Pl. 26.

Common Harrier.

Drawn from Nature by J.J.Audubon,F.R.S.F.L.S. Lith.d Printed & Col.d by J. T. Bowen, Philad.

No. 7. Pl. 31.

Burrowing Day-Owl.

Drawn from Nature by J. J. Audubon, F.R.S. F.L.S.

Lith.d Printed & Col.d by J. T. Bowen, Philad.a

No. 6. Pl. 30.

Columbian Day Owl.

Drawn from Nature by J. J. Audubon, F.R.S. F.L.S.

Lith.d Printed & Col.d by J. T. Bowen, Philad.a

No 6 Pl. 27.

Hawk Owl.

Drawn from Nature by J. J. Audubon, F.R.S.F.L.S. Lith.d Printed & Col.d by J. T. Bowen, Philad.a

Passerine Day-Owl.

Drawn from Nature by J.J.Audubon. F.R.S.F.L.S.

Lith. Printed & Col. by J.T.Bowen. Philada.

R.T.

Snowy Owl.

Drawn from Nature by J. J. Audubon, F.R.S. F.L.S.

Lith^{d} Printed & Col^{d} by J. T. Bowen, Philad^{a}

No. 7. Pl. 33.

Little or Acadian Owl

Common Mouse

Drawn from Nature by J.J.Audubon, F.R.S.F.L.S. Lith.d Printed & Col.d by J. T. Bowen, Philad.a

No 7. Pl. 32.

Tengmalm's Night-Owl.

Drawn from Nature by J. J. Audubon, F.R.S.F.L.S. Lith^d Printed & Col^d by J. T. Bowen, Philad^a

No. 7. Pl. 34

Barn Owl.

Drawn from Nature by J.J. Audubon, F.R.S.F.L.S. Lith.d Printed & Col.d by J. T. Bowen, Philad.a

Barred Owl.

Drawn from Nature by J.J. Audubon, F.R.S.F.L.S. Lith.d Printed & Col.d by J. T. Bowen, Philad.a

Great Cinereous Owl.

Drawn from Nature by J.J.Audubon,F.R.S.F.L.S.

Lith.d Printed & Col.d by J. T. Bowen, Philad.a

No. 8. Pl. 37.

Long-eared Owl.

Drawn from Nature by J.J. Audubon, F.R.S. F.L.S.

Lith.d Printed & Col.d by J.T. Bowen, Philad.a

Short-eared Owl.

Drawn from Nature by J.J.Audubon F.R.S.F.L.S. Lithd Printed & Cold by J.T. Bowen. Philada

Little Screech Owl.
Jersey Pine. Pinus inops

Drawn from Nature by J. J. Audubon F.R.S. F.L.S.

Lith.d Printed & Col.d by J. T. Bowen. Philad.a

No. 8. Pl. 39.

Great Horned-Owl.

Drawn from Nature by J.J.Audubon, F.R.S.F.L.S.

Lith.d Printed & Col.d by J. T. Bowen, Philad.a

Chuck-will's Widow,
(Harlequin Snake)

Drawn from Nature by J. J. Audubon, F.R.S. F.L.S.

Lith.d Printed & Col.d by J. T. Bowen, Philad.a

No. 99. Pl. 495.

Nuttall's Whip-poor-will

Male

Drawn from Nature by J. J. Audubon F.R.S. F.L.S. Lith. Printed & Col^d by J. T. Bowen, Philad^a

No. 9. Pl. 42

Whip-poor-will

Black Oak or Quercitron. Quercus tinctoria.

Drawn from Nature by J.J.Audubon, F.R.S.F.L.S.

Lith.d Printed & Col.d by J. T. Bowen, Philad.a

No. 9 Pl. 43

Night Hawk.

White Oak. Quercus Alba.

Drawn from Nature by J. J. Audubon, F.R.S. F.L.S.

Lith.d Printed & Col.d by J. T. Bowen, Philad.a

American Swift.
(Nests.)

Drawn from Nature by J. J. Audubon. F.R.S.F.L.S.

Lith.d Printed & Col.d by J. T. Bowen. Philad.a

Bank Swallow

Drawn from Nature by J. J. Audubon. F.R.S.F.L.S.

Lith.d Printed & Col.d by J. T. Bowen. Philad.a

No. 10. Pl. 48.

Barn or Chimney Swallow.

Drawn from Nature by J. J. Audubon F.R.S. F.L. Lith.d Printed & Col.d by J. T. Bowen, Philad.a

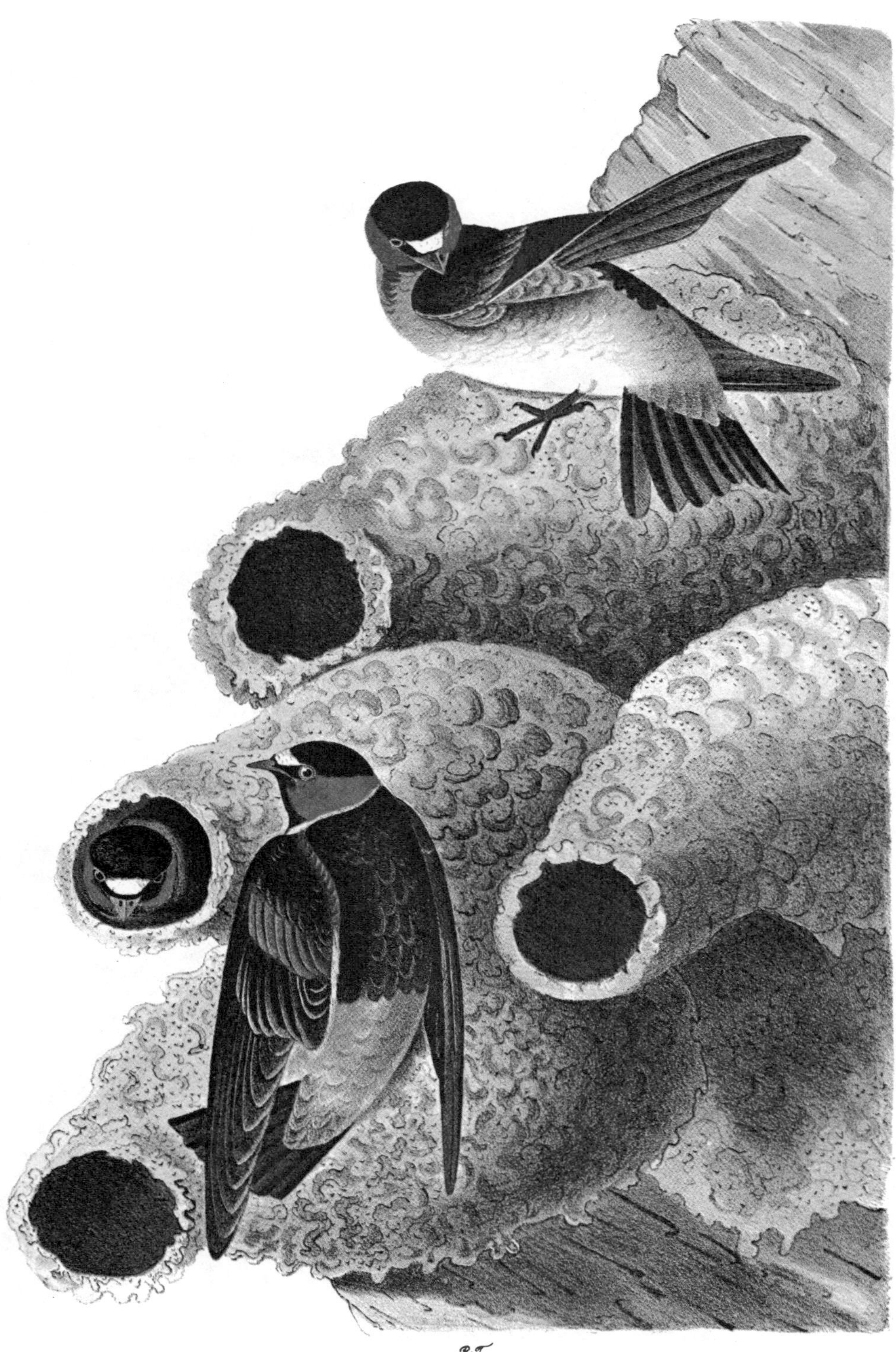

Cliff Swallow.
(Nests.)

Drawn from Nature by J. J. Audubon, F.R.S.F.L.S.

Lith^d. Printed & Col^d. by J. T. Bowen, Philad^a.

No. 9.

Pl. 45.

Purple Martin.
(Calabash.)

Drawn from Nature by J.J.Audubon.F.R.S.F.L.S.

Lith.d Printed & Col.d by J.T.Bowen.Philad.a

Rough-winged Swallow.

Drawn from Nature by J.J. Audubon. F.R.S.F.L.S. Lith^d Printed & Col^d by J.T. Bowen. Philad^a

No. 10. Pl. 49.

R. 9

Violet-Green Swallow.

Drawn from Nature by J.J. Audubon F.R.S.F.L.S.

Lithd. Printed & Cold. by J.T. Bowen, Philada.

No. 10. Pl. 46.

White-bellied Swallow.

Drawn from Nature by J.J.Audubon. F.R.S.F.L.S. Lith.^d Printed & Col.^d by J.T. Bowen. Philad.^a

American Redstart

Virginian Hornbeam or Iron-wood Tree.

1. Male 2. Female.

Drawn from Nature by J.J.Audubon, F.R.S.F.L.S. Lith.d Printed & Col.d by J. T. Bowen, Philad.a

N°. 11

Pl. 54

R.T.

Arkansaw Flycatcher.

Drawn from Nature by J. J. Audubon, F.R.S. F.L.S.

Lith^d Printed & Col^d by J. T. Bowen, Philad^a

Cooper's Flycatcher.
(Balsam or Silver Fir. Pinus Balsamea.)

1 Male. 2 Female.

Drawn from Nature by J.J.Audubon, F.R.S.F.L.S. Lith.d Printed & Col.d by J.T.Bowen. Philad.a

No. 12 Pl. 57

Great Crested Flycatcher.

Drawn from Nature by J. J. Audubon. F.R.S. F.L.S. Lith.d Printed & Col.d by J. T. Bowen, Philad.a

No. 99. Pl. 491.

R.T.

Least Flycatcher

Male

Drawn from Nature by J. J. Audubon, F.R.S. F.L.S. Lith. Printed & Col.d by J. T. Bowen, Philad.a

N°14 Pl 166

Least Pewee Flycatcher.
White Oak. Quercus Prinus.

Male.

Drawn from Nature by J.J.Audubon, F.R.S.F.L.S. Lith.d Printed & Col.d by J.T.Bowen, Philad.a

Pewee Flycatcher.

Cotton Plant. Gossypium. Herbaceum.

1 Male 2 Female

Drawn from Nature by J.J. Audubon. F.R.S.F.L.S.

Lith^d. Printed & Col^d. by J.T. Bowen. Philad^a.

No. 11.

Pl. 55.

Pipiry Flycatcher.

Agati Grandiflora.

Drawn from Nature by J.J.Audubon. F.R.S.F.L.S.

Lith.d Printed & Col.d by J.T.Bowen. Philad.a

No 12. Pl. 60.

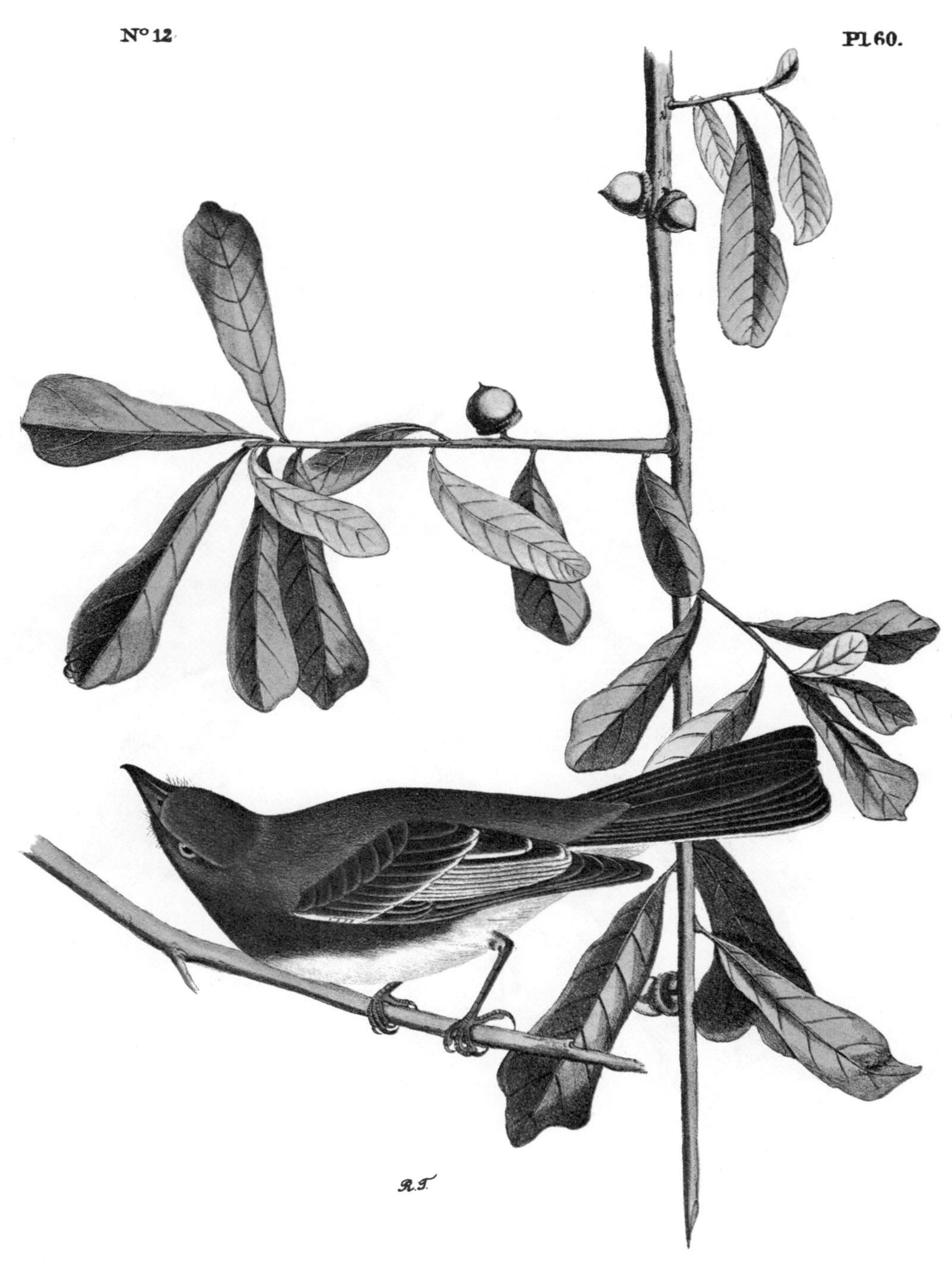

R.T.

Rocky Mountain Flycatcher.
(Swamp Oak. Quercus Aquatica.)
Male

Drawn from Nature by J. J. Audubon. F.R.S.F.L.S.

Lith.d Printed & Col.d by J. T. Bowen, Philad.a

N°12. Pl.59.

Say's Flycatcher.

1. Male. 2. Female.

Drawn from Nature by J.J.Audubon.F.R.S.F.L.S.

Lithd Printed & Cold by J.T.Bowen.Philada

No. 13 Pl. 62

Small Green-crested Flycatcher.

Sassafras. Laurus Sassafras

1 Male. 2 Female.

Drawn from Nature by J.J. Audubon. F.R.S.F.L.S. Lith^{d}. Printed & Col^{d}. by J.T. Bowen. Philad^{a}.

No. 13 Pl. 61.

R.T.

Short-legged Pewit Flycatcher.
(Hobble Bush. Viburnum Lantanoides)

Male

Drawn from Nature by J. J. Audubon. F.R.S. F.L.S. Lith.d Printed & Col.d by J. T. Bowen. Philad.a

Small-headed Flycatcher

Virginian Spider-wort. Tradescantia virginica.

Male

Drawn from Nature by J.J.Audubon.F.R.S.F.L.S.

Lith.d Printed & Col.d by J.T.Bowen. Phila.

No. 13. Pl 65.

Traill's Flycatcher
Sweet Gum. Liquidambar Styraciflua.

Male

Drawn from Nature by J. J. Audubon F.R.S.F.L.S. | Lith.d Printed & Col.d by J. T. Bowen Philad.a

No. 12

Pl. 56.

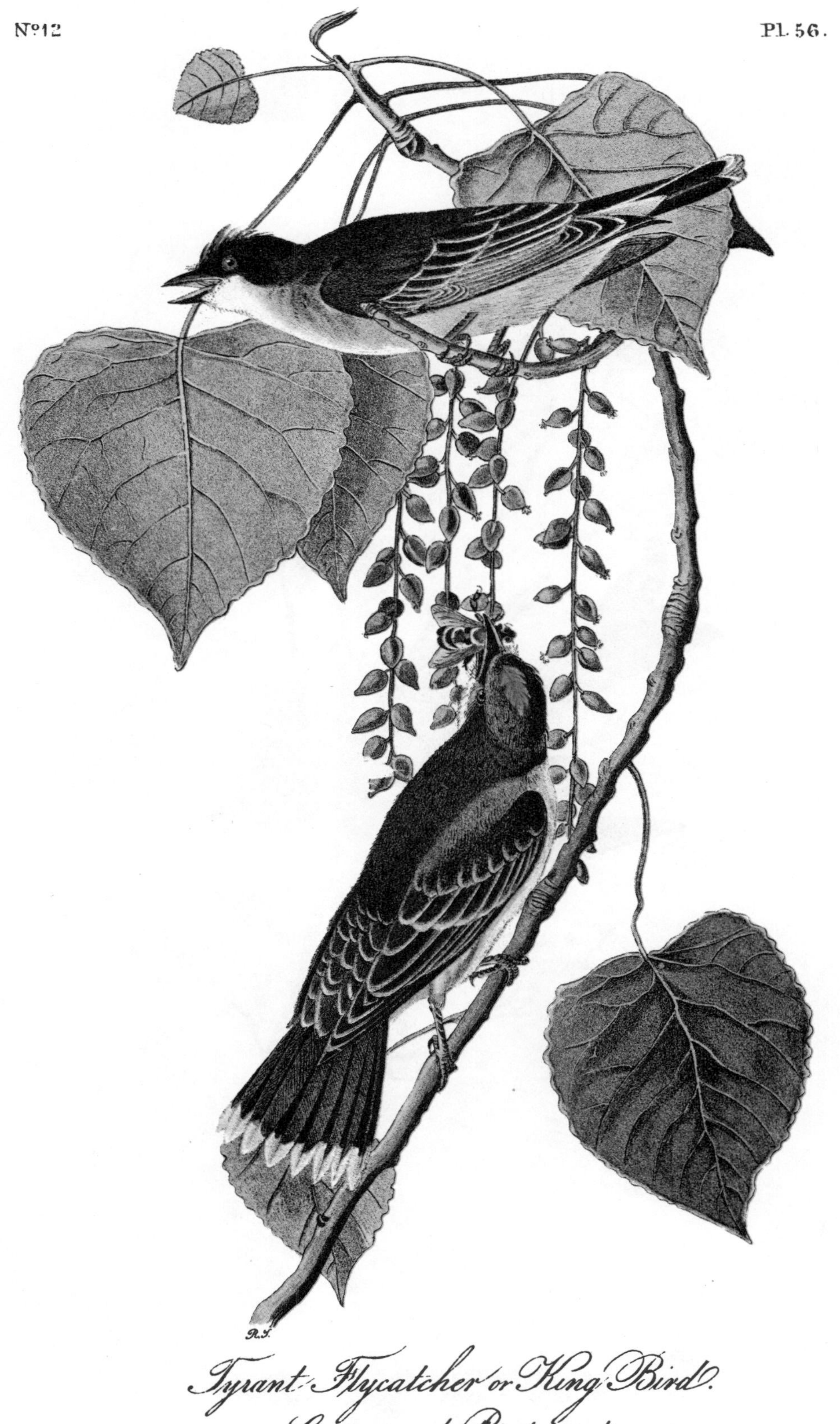

R. T.

Tyrant Flycatcher or King Bird.

Cotton-wood. Populus candicans.

Drawn from Nature by J. J. Audubon, F.R.S.F.L.S.

Lith.d Printed & Col.d by J. T. Bowen, Philad.a

Wood Pewee Flycatcher
Swamp Honeysuckle. Azalea Viscosa.

Male

Drawn from Nature by J. J. Audubon. F.R.S.F.L.S.

Lith^{d} Printed & Col^{d} by J. T. Bowen. Philad^{a}

No. 98 Pl. 490.

W.E.H.

Yellow-bellied Flycatcher

Male

Drawn from Nature by J. J. Audubon, F.R.S. F.L.S

Lith. Printed & Col.d by J. T. Bowen, Philada.

No 11. Pl. 52.

Fork-tailed Flycatcher.

Gordonia Lasianthus.

Drawn from Nature by J.J. Audubon. F.R.S.F.L.S. Lithd Printed & Cold by J.T. Bowen. Philada

No. 11. Pl. 53.

Swallow-tailed Flycatcher.

Drawn from Nature by J. J. Audubon. F.R.S. F.L.S.

Lith.d Printed & Col.d by J. T. Bowen. Philad.a

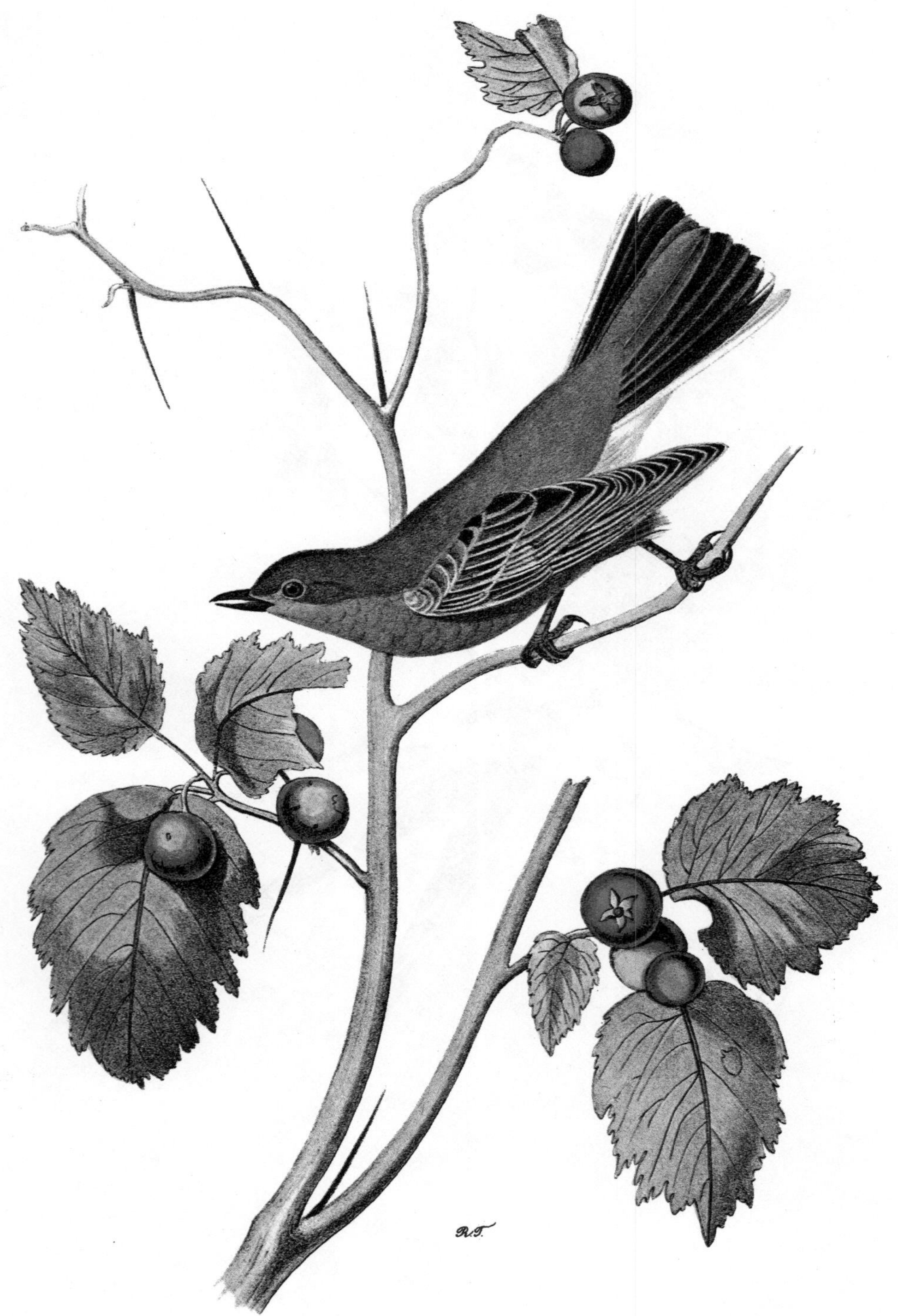

Townsend's Ptilogonys.

Female.

Drawn from Nature by J.J.Audubon F.R.S.F.L.S.

Lith.d Printed & Col.d by J.T. Bowen Philad.a

No. 14 Pl. 70.

Blue-grey Flycatcher.

Black Walnut. Juglans nigra.

1. Male. 2. Female.

Drawn from Nature by J. J. Audubon, F.R.S.F.L.S.

Lith.d Printed & Col.d by J. T. Bowen, Philad.a

Bonaparte's Flycatching-Warbler.
Great Magnolia. Magnolia Grandiflora.
Male.

Drawn from Nature by J.J.Audubon.F.R.S.F.L.S.

Lith.d Printed & Col.d by J.T.Bowen, Philad.a

No. 15 Pl. 72

Canada Flycatcher.
Great Laurel Rhododendron maximum

1. Male 2. Female.

Drawn from Nature by J. J. Audubon, F.R.S.F.L.S.

Lith.d Printed & Col.d by J. T. Bowen, Philad.a

No. 15

Pl. 71

Hooded Flycatching Warbler.

(Erithrypa herbacea.)

1. Male. 2. Female.

Drawn from Nature by J.J. Audubon. F.R.S.F.L.S

Lith.d Printed & Col.d by J.T. Bowen, Philad.a

N° 15

Pl. 74

Kentucky Flycatching-Warbler.
Magnolia auriculata.

1 Male. 2 Female.

Drawn from Nature by J. J. Audubon F.R.S.F.L.S.

Lith.d Printed & Col.d by J. T. Bowen, Philad.a

No. 15 Pl. 75.

Wilson's Flycatching-Warbler.

Snakes' Head. Chelone Glabra.

1. Male. 2. Female.

Drawn from Nature by J. J. Audubon, F.R.S. F.L.S.

Lith.d Printed & Col.d by J. T. Bowen, Philad.a

Audubon's Wood-Warbler.
Strawberry Tree. Euonymus Americanus.
1. Male. 2 Female.

Drawn from Nature by J.J.Audubon.F.R.S.F.L.S.

Lith.d Printed & Col.d by J.T Bowen. Philad.a

No. 16. Pl. 80.

Bay-breasted Wood-Warbler

Highland Cotton-plant. Gossipium herbaceum.

1. Male. 2. Female.

Drawn from Nature by J. J. Audubon. F.R.S.F.L.S.

Lith.d Printed & Col.d by J. T. Bowen. Philad.a

No. 20 Pl. 96.

Black & yellow Wood-Warbler.

1. Male. 2. Female. 3. Young.

Flowering Raspberry. Rubus odoratus.

Drawn from Nature by J.J. Audubon, F.R.S.F.L.S. Lith.d Printed & Col.d by J.T. Bowen, Philad.a

Blackburnian Wood-Warbler

1. Male. 2. Female.

Phlox maculata.

Drawn from Nature by J.J.Audubon. F.R.S.F.L.S.

Lith.d Printed & Col.d by J.T. Bowen, Philad.a

Black-poll Wood Warbler.

Black Gum Tree. Nyssa aquatica.

1. Males. 2 Female.

Drawn from Nature by J.J. Audubon. F.R.S.F.L.S.

Lith.d Printed & Col.d by J.T. Bowen. Philad.a

No 19 Pl. 95.

Black-throated Blue Wood-Warbler

1. Male 2. Female.

Canadian Columbine

Drawn from Nature by J. J. Audubon, F.R.S.F.L.S. Lith.d Printed & Col.d by J. T. Bowen, Philad.a

Black-throated Green Wood Warbler.

Caprifolium Sempervirens

1 Male 2 Female.

Drawn from Nature by J.J.Audubon F.R.S.F.L.S. Lith.d Printed & Col.d by J.T. Bowen, Philad.a

Black-throated Grey Wood-Warbler.

Males.

Drawn from Nature by J. J. Audubon, F.R.S.F.L.S. Lith. Printed & Col. by J. T. Bowen, Philad.

No. 20. Pl. 98.

Blue Mountain Warbler.

Male

Drawn from Nature by J.J.Audubon.F.R.S.F.L.S. Lith.d Printed & Col.d by J.T.Bowen.Philad.a

Blue yellow-backed Wood-Warbler.

1. Male. 2. Female.

Louisiana Flag.

Drawn from Nature by J.J.Audubon. F.R.S.F.L.S.

Lith.d Printed & Col.d by J.T. Bowen. Philad.a

Cape May Wood-Warbler.

1. Male 2. Female.

Drawn from Nature by J.J.Audubon, F.R.S.F.L.S.

Lith.d Printed & Col.d by J.T. Bowen, Philad.a

No 17. Pl. 81.

Chesnut-sided Wood Warbler.

Moth Mullein. Verbascum Blattaria.

1. Male. 2. Female.

Drawn from Nature by J. J. Audubon, F.R.S. F.L.S.

Lith.d Printed & Col.d by J. T. Bowen Philad.a

Cærulean Wood-Warbler.

1. Old Male. 2. Young Male.

Bear-berry and Spanish Mulberry.

Drawn from Nature by J. J. Audubon, F.R.S. F.L.S.

Lith.d Printed & Col.d by J. T. Bowen, Philad.a

No. 20 Pl. 99.

Connecticut Warbler.

1. Male. 2. Female.

Gentiana Saponaria.

Drawn from Nature by J. J. Audubon, F.R.S. F.L.S.

Lith. Printed & Col. by J. T. Bowen, Philad.

R. T.

Hemlock Warbler

Dwarf Maple. Acer Spicatum

1. Male 2. Female.

Drawn from Nature by J. J. Audubon. F.R.S.F.L.S.

Lith.d Printed & Col.d by J. T. Bowen. Philad.a

No. 19. Pl. 93.

Hermit Wood-Warbler.

1. Male 2. Female.

Strawberry Tree.

Drawn from Nature by J.J.Audubon, F.R.S.F.L.S. Lith^d Printed & Col^d by J.T. Bowen, Philad^a

No. 17. Pl. 82.

Pine-creeping Wood-Warbler

Yellow Pine. Pinus variabilis.

1. Male 2. Female.

Drawn from Nature by J.J.Audubon.F.R.S.F.L.S.

Lithd. Printed & Cold. by J.T.Bowen.Philada.

Prairie Wood-Warbler.

1. Male. 2. Female.

Buffalo Grass.

Drawn from Nature by J. J. Audubon. F.R.S.F.L.S.

Lith.d Printed & Col.d by J. T. Bowen. Philad.a

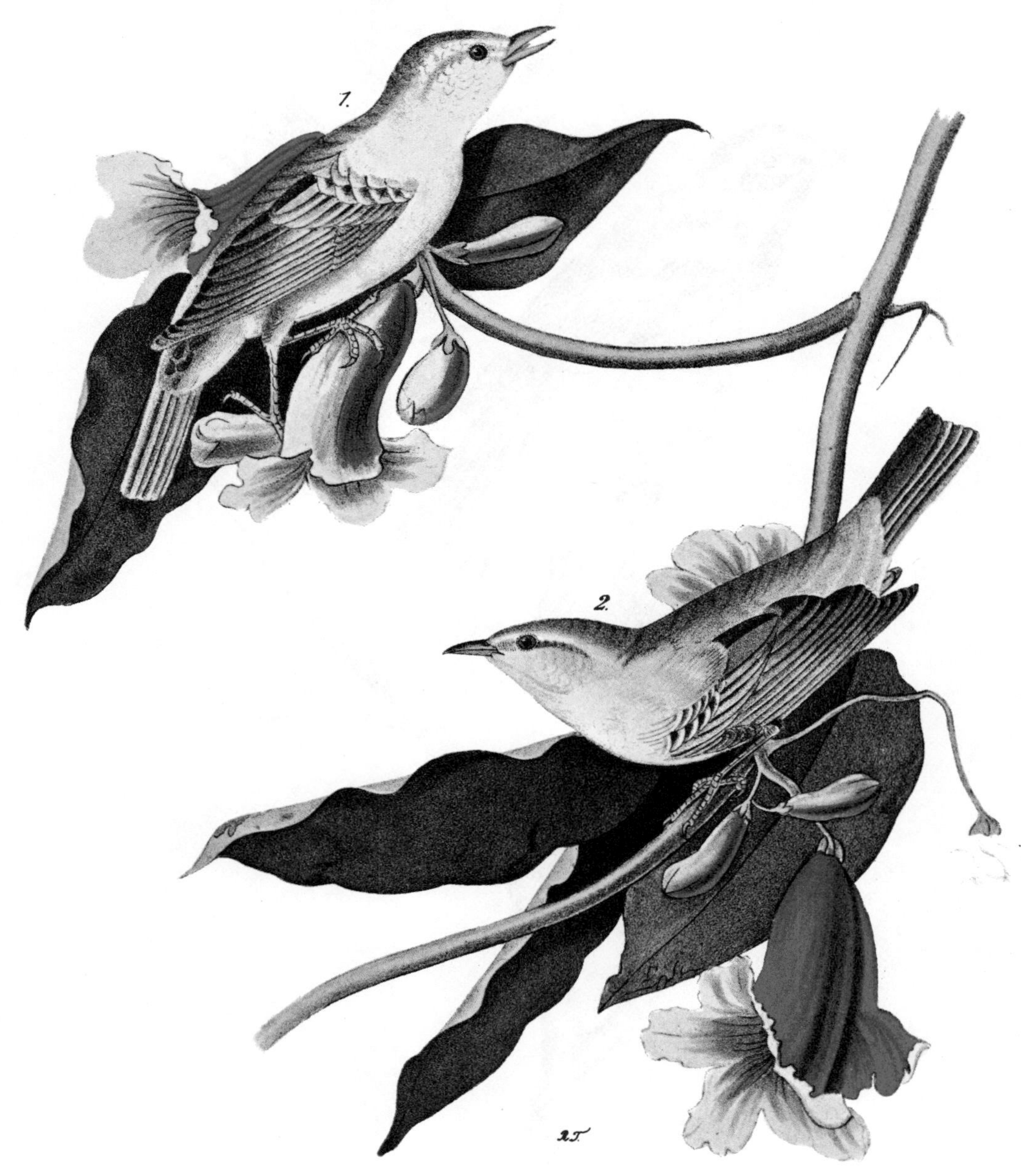

Rathbone's Wood-Warbler.

1 Male. 2 Female.

Ramping Trumpet-flower?

Drawn from Nature by J. J. Audubon. F.R.S.F.L.S.

Lith^d. Printed & Col^d. by J.T. Bowen. Philad^a.

No. 19 Pl. 92.

R.T.

Townsend's Wood-Warbler.

Male.

Carolina Allspice.

Drawn from Nature by J.J.Audubon, F.R.S.F.L.S

Lithd. Printed & Cold. by J.T. Bowen, Philada.

Yellow-crowned Wood-Warbler.

Iris versicolor.

1. Male 2. Young.

Drawn from Nature by J.J.Audubon.F.R.S.F.L.S.

Lith.d Printed & Col.d by J.T.Bowen.Philad.a

No. 18. Pl. 88.

Yellow-poll Wood-Warbler.

Males.

Drawn from Nature by J. J. Audubon, F.R.S. F.L.S. Lith.[d] Printed & Col.[d] by J. T. Bowen, Philad.[a]

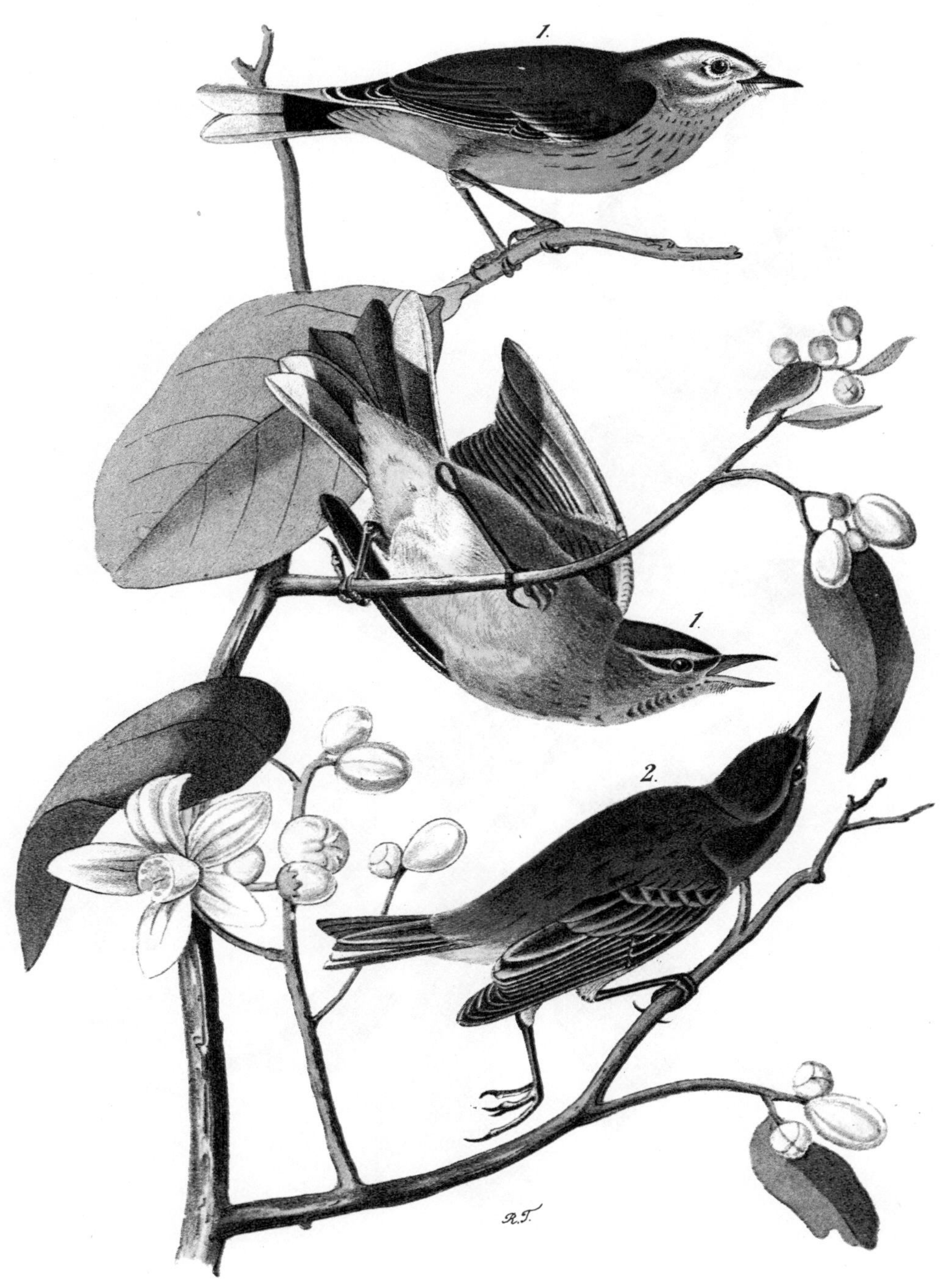

Yellow Red-poll Wood-Warbler.

1. Males 2. Young.

Wild Orange Tree

Drawn from Nature by J. J. Audubon, F.R.S. F.L.S.

Lith.d Printed & Col.d by J. T. Bowen, Philad.a

R. T.

Yellow-throated Wood-Warbler.

Chinquapin. Castanea pumila.

Male.

Drawn from Nature by J. J. Audubon. F.R.S.F.L.S.

Lith.d Printed & Col.d by J. T. Bowen, Philad.a

No. 21.

Pl. 103.

R.T.

Delafield's Ground-Warbler.

Male.

Drawn from Nature by J. J. Audubon. F.R.S.F.L.S.

Lithd. Printed & Cold. by J. T. Bowen, Philada.

Macgillivray's Ground-Warbler

1. Male. 2. Female.

Drawn from Nature by J. J. Audubon. F.R.S.F.L.S. Lith.d Printed & Col.d by J. T. Bowen. Philad.a

No. 21. Pl. 102.

Maryland Ground-Warbler.

1. Adult Male. 2. Young Male. 3. Female.

Bitter-wood Tree. Viburnum prunifolium.

Drawn from Nature by J. J. Audubon, F.R.S. F.L.S. Lith.d Printed & Col.d by J. T. Bowen, Philad.a

No. 21 Pl. 101

Mourning Ground-Warbler.

Male.

Pheasant's-eye Flos-Adonis.

Drawn from Nature by J. J. Audubon, F.R.S. F.L.S. Lith.d Printed & Col.d by J. T. Bowen, Philad.a

No. 22. Pl. 108.

Bachman's Swamp-Warbler.

1. Male. 2. Female

Gordonia pubescens.

Drawn from Nature by J. J. Audubon. F.R.S. F.L.S. Lith.d Printed & Col.d by J. T. Bowen. Philad.a

No. 23. Pl. 111.

R.T.

Blue-winged Yellow Swamp-Warbler.

1. Male 2. Female

Cotton Rose. Hibiscus grandiflorus.

Drawn from Nature by J.J.Audubon.F.R.S.F.L.S.

Lith.d Printed & Col.d by J.T.Bowen.Philad.a

No. 22. Pl. 109.

R.T.

Carbonated Swamp-Warbler

Males

May-bush or Service. Pyrus Botryapium.

Drawn from Nature by J.J. Audubon, F.R.S. F.L.S. Lith.d Printed & Col.d by J.T. Bowen, Philad.a

R.T.

Golden-winged Swamp-Warbler.

1. Male. 2. Female.

Drawn from Nature by J. J. Audubon, F.R.S.F.L.S. Lith^d. Printed & Col^d. by J. T. Bowen, Philad^a.

N° 23.
Pl. 113.
2.
1.
R.T.
Nashville Swamp Warbler
1. Male. 2. Female
Swamp Spice Ilex Prinoides
Drawn from Nature by J. J. Audubon, F.R.S. F.L.S.
Lith.d Printed & Col.d by J. T. Bowen, Philad.a

No. 23. Pl. 112.

Orange-crowned Swamp-Warbler.

1. Male 2. Female.

Huckleberry. Vaccinium frondosum.

Drawn from Nature by J. J. Audubon. F.R.S.F.L.S.

Lith.d Printed & Col.d by J. T. Bowen, Philad.a

No. 22.

Pl. 106.

R.T.

Prothonotary Swamp-Warbler.

1. Male. 2. Female.

Cane Vine

Drawn from Nature by J. J. Audubon, F.R.S. F.L.S.

Lithd. Printed & Cold. by J. T. Bowen, Philada.

No. 21 Pl. 104

R. T.

Swainson's Swamp Warbler.

Male.

Orange-coloured Azalea. Azalea calendulacea.

Drawn from Nature by J. J. Audubon. F.R.S.F.L.S. Lith.d Printed & Col.d by J. T. Bowen. Philad.a

No. 22. Pl. 110.

Tennessee Swamp Warbler.

Male

Ilex laxiflora

Drawn from Nature by J.J.Audubon.F.R.S.F.L.S.

Lith[d] Printed & Col[d] by J.T.Bowen.Philad[a]

No. 21 Pl. 105

Worm-eating Swamp Warbler.

1. Male. 2. Female.

American Poke-weed. Phytolacca decandra.

Drawn from Nature by J. J. Audubon, F.R.S.F.L.S.

Lithd. Printed & Cold. by J. T. Bowen, Philada.

No. 23. Pl. 114.

R.T.

Black-and-white Creeping Warbler

Male.

Black Larch. Pinus pendula.

Drawn from Nature by J. J. Audubon. F.R.S.F.L.S.

Lith.d Printed & Col.d by J. T. Bowen. Philad.a

No. 23. Pl. 115.

R.T.

Brown Tree-creeper

1 Male 2 Female

Drawn from Nature by J.J.Audubon.F.R.S.F.L.S. Lith.d Printed & Col.d by J.T.Bowen.Philad.a

Bewicks Wren

Male.

Iron-wood Tree

Drawn from Nature by J. J. Audubon. F.R.S.F.L.S.

Lith.d Printed & Col.d by J. T. Bowen. Philad.a

Great Carolina Wren.

1. Male. 2. Female.

Dwarf Buck-eye. Æsculus. Pavia.

Drawn from Nature by J.J.Audubon, F.R.S.F.L.S.

Lith.d Printed & Col.d by J. T. Bowen, Philad.a

No. 25. Pl. 123.

Marsh Wren

1. Males 2 Female and Nest

Drawn from Nature by J. J. Audubon F.R.S F.L.S

Lith. Printed & Col. by J. T. Bowen, Philad.

No. 24 Pl. 120

R.T.

House Wren

1. Male. 2. Female. 3. Young.

In an old Hat.

Drawn from Nature by J.J. Audubon, F.R.S. F.L.S.

Lith.d Printed & Col.d by J.T. Bowen, Philad.a

Parkman's Wren.

Male.

Pogonia divaricata

Drawn from Nature by J. J. Audubon F.R.S. F.L.S.

Lith.d Printed & Col.d by J. T. Bowen, Philad.a

No. 24 Pl. 116.

R.T.

Rock - Wren

Adult Female

Smilacina borealis

Drawn from Nature by J. J. Audubon. F.R.S.F.L.S.

Lith.d Printed & Col.d by J. T. Bowen, Philad.a

No. 25. Pl. 124

R.T.

Short-billed Marsh Wren.

1. Male. 2. Female and Nest.

Drawn from Nature by J.J. Audubon F.R.S. F.L.S. Lith.d Printed & Col.d by J.T. Bowen, Philad.a

Winter Wren.

1. Male. 2. Female. 3. Young

Drawn from Nature by J. J. Audubon F.R.S.F.L.S.

Lithd. Printed & Cold. by J. T. Bowen, Philada.

No. 24. Pl. 119.

Wood Wren

Male.

Arbutus. Uva-ursi

Drawn from Nature by J. J. Audubon, F.R.S.F.L.S.

Lith.d Printed & Col.d by J. T. Bowen, Philad.a

No. 26.

Pl 126.

R.T.

Black cap Titmouse

1. Male 2. Female.

Sweet briar?.—

Drawn from Nature by J.J.Audubon F.R.S.L.L.S.

Lith.d Printed & Col.d by J.T. Bowen Phila.

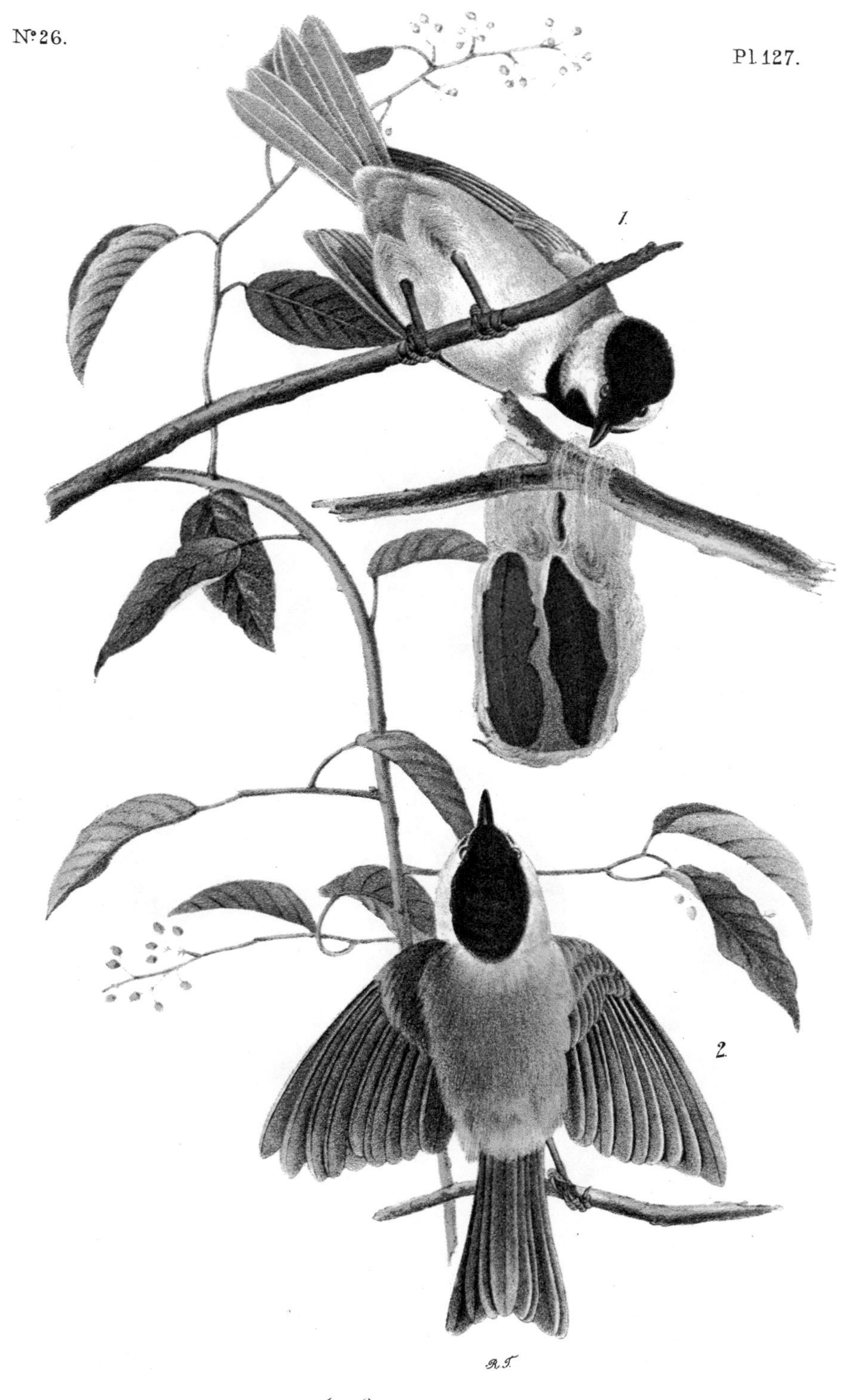

Carolina Titmouse.

1. Male. 2. Female.

Plant. Supple Jack.

Drawn from Nature by J. J. Audubon F.R.S.F.L.S.

Lith^d. Printed & Col^d. by J. T. Bowen. Philad^a.

Chesnut-backed Titmouse.

1. Male. 2. Female.

No. 26. Pl. 130.

Chesnut-crowned Titmouse

1. Male. 2. Female and Nest.

Drawn from Nature by J. J. Audubon. F.R.S.F.L.S.

Lith.d Printed & Col.d by J. T. Bowen. Philad.a

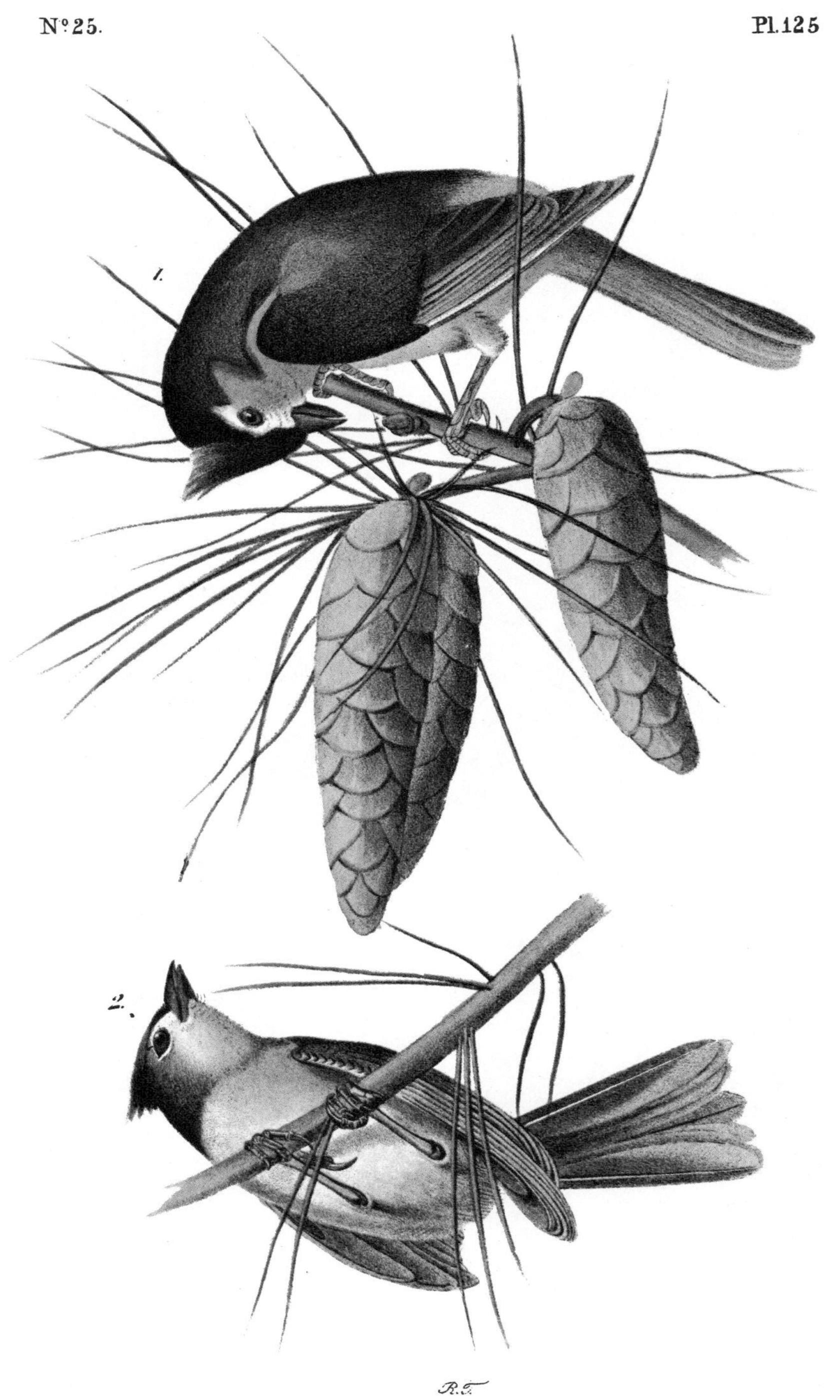

Crested Titmouse

1. Male 2. Female.

White Pine. Pinus Strobus

Drawn from Nature by J. J. Audubon, F.R.S. F.L.S.

Lith^d. Printed & Col^d. by J. T. Bowen, Philad^a.

No. 26. Pl. 128.

1.

2.

3.

R.T.

Hudson's Bay Titmouse.

1. Male. 2. Female. 3. Young.

Drawn from Nature by J. J. Audubon F.R.S.F.L.S.

Lith.d Printed & Col.d by J. T. Bowen Philad.a

No. 27. Pl. 132

R.T.

American Golden-crested Kinglet.

1. Male 2. Female.

Thalia dealbata.

Drawn from Nature by J.J. Audubon. F.R.S.F.L.S. — Lith.d Printed & Col.d by J.T. Bowen. Philad.a

R.T.

Cuvier's Kinglet

Male.

Broad-leaved laurel. Kalmia latifolia.

Drawn from Nature by J.J.Audubon, F.R.S.F.L.S.

Lith[d] Printed & Col[d] by J.T. Bowen, Philad[a]

Ruby-crowned Kinglet

1. Male. 2. Female.

Kalmia augustifolia.

Drawn from Nature by J. J. Audubon, F.R.S.F.L.S.

Lith^d Printed & Col^d by J. T. Bowen, Philad^a

No. 28. Pl. 136

Arctic Blue Bird
Male 1. Female 2

Drawn from nature by J.J. Audubon F.R.S.F.L.S. Lith & Printed by Endicott New York.

Common Blue Bird

1. Male. 2. Female. 3 Young.

Great Mullein Verbascum Thapsus.

Drawn from Nature by J. J. Audubon. F.R.S.F.L.S. Lith.d Printed & Col.d by J. T. Bowen, Philad.a

Western Blue Bird.

1. Male. 2. Female.

Drawn from Nature by J.J.Audubon.F.R.S.F.L.S.

Lith.d Printed & Col.d by J.T.Bowen.Philad.a

Drawn from nature by J.J. Audubon F.R.S. F.L.S.

Lith.d Printed by Endicott New York

American Dipper
Male 1. Female 2.

No. 28. Pl. 140.

Cat Bird
Male 1 Female 2.
Plant Black-berry, Rubus villosus.

Drawn from nature by J. J. Audubon F.R.S.F.L.S. Lith. & Printed by Endicott New York.

No. 28. Pl. 138.

Common Mocking Bird
Males 1 & 2 Female 3,
Florida Jessamine, Gelseminum niditum
Rattlesnake

Drawn from nature by J.J. Audubon F.R.S.F.L.S. Lith. & Printed by Endicott New York.

Ferruginous Mocking Bird
Males 1, 2, 3, Female 4.

Drawn from nature by J.J. Audubon F.R.S.F.L.S. Lith & Printed by Endicott New York

No. 28 Pl. 139.

Mountain Mocking Bird.
Male.

Drawn from nature by J.J. Audubon F.R.S.F.L.S. Lith. & Printed by Endicott New York.

American Robin, or Migratory Thrush.
Male 1. Female 2 and young
Chesnut Oak Quercus prinus.

Drawn from nature by J.J. Audubon F.R.S.F.L.S. Lith. & Printed by Endicott New York

Dwarf Thrush
Male

Plant Porcelia Triloba.

Drawn from nature by J.J. Audubon F.R.S.F.L.S.

Lith. & Printed by Endicott New York

Hermit Thrush

Male 1. Female 2.

Plant Robin Wood.

Drawn from nature by J.J. Audubon F.R.S.F.L.S. Lith. & Printed by Endicott New York.

No. 29. Pl. 145.

Tawny Thrush,
Male,

Habenaria Lacera – Cornus Canadensis

Drawn from nature by J.J. Audubon F.R.S.F.L.S. Lith. & Printed by Endicott New York

Varied Thrush.
Male 1, Female 2.
American Mistletoe, Viscum verticillatum.

Drawn from nature by J.J. Audubon F.R.S.F.L.S.

Lith. & Printed by Endicott New York.

Wood Thrush
Male 1. Female 2.
Common Dogwood.

Drawn from nature by J.J. Audubon F.R.S.F.L.S. Lith. & Printed by Endicott New York

N°. 30. Pl. 149.

Aquatic Wood-Wagtail

Male 1 Female 2.

Plant. Indian Turnip.

Drawn from nature by J.J. Audubon F.R.S.F.L.S. Lith & Printed by Endicott New York

Golden Crowned Wagtail (Thrush.)
Male 1. Female 2.
Plant Woody Nightshade.

Drawn from nature by J.J. Audubon F.R.S.F.L.S. Lith. & Printed by Endicott New York

1

2

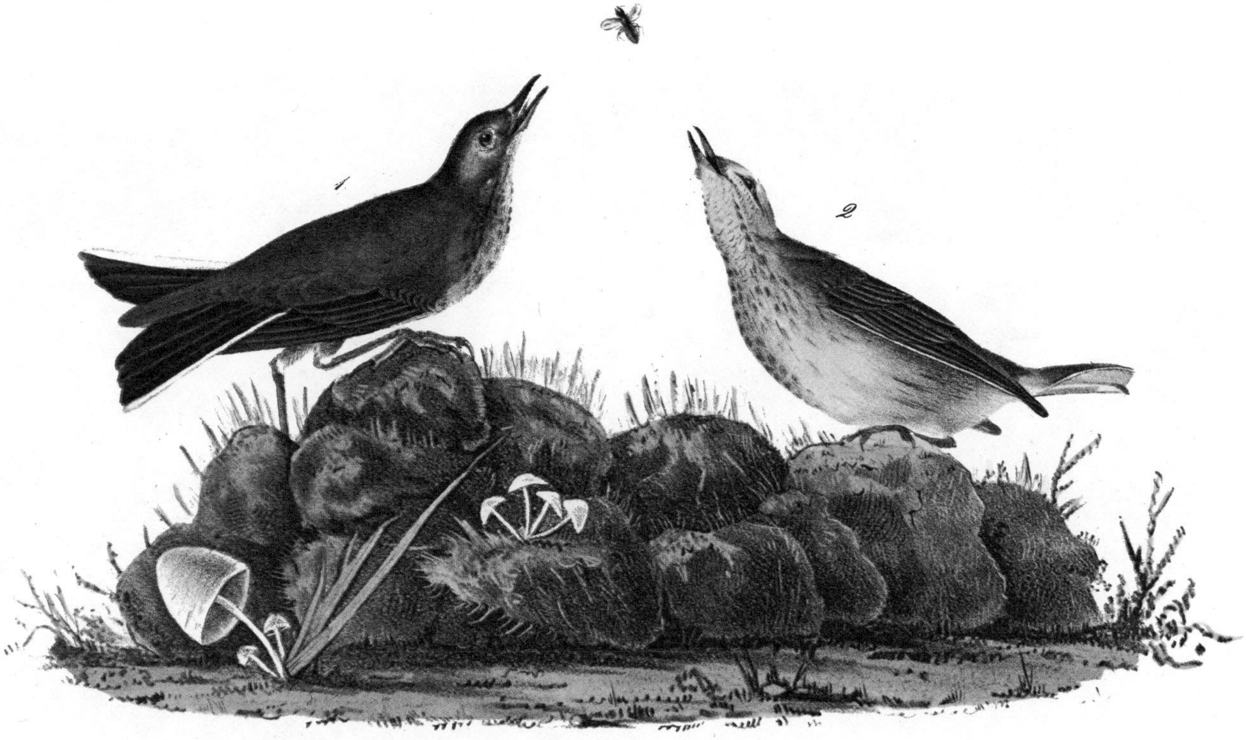

American Pipit or Titlark.

Male 1 Female 2.

Drawn from nature by J.J. Audubon F.R.S.F.L.S.

Lith. & Printed by Endicott New York

N°. 31.
Pl. 151
Shore Lark
1 Male Summer Plumage 2. Do Winter 3. Female 4 Young & Nest
Drawn from Nature by J. J. Audubon, F.R.S.F.L.S.
Lith.d Printed & Col.d by J. T. Bowen, Philad.a

No. 98. Pl. 486.

W.E.H.

Sprague's Missouri Lark

Male.

Drawn from Nature by J. J. Audubon, F.R.S. F.L.S.

Lith. Printed & Col.d by J. T. Bowen, Phila.

No.100. Pl.497.

W.E.H.

Western Shore Lark

Male

Drawn from Nature by J. J. Audubon, F.R.S. F.L.S.

Lith. Printed & Col.d by J. T. Bowen, Philada.

R.T.

Chesnut-collared Lark-Bunting.

Male.

Drawn from Nature by J.J.Audubon.F.R.S.F.L.S.

Lith.d Printed & Col.d by J.T.Bowen.Philad.a

No 31. Pl. 152.

Lapland Lark Bunting.

1. Male Spring Plumage 2. Do Winter. 3. Female.

Drawn from Nature by J. J. Audubon F.R.S.F.L.S.

Lith. Printed & Col.d by J. T. Bowen, Philad.a

R.T.

Painted Lark-Bunting.

Male.

Drawn from Nature by J. J. Audubon F.R.S.F.L.S.

Lith.d Printed & Col.d by J. T. Bowen Philad.a

No. 98. Pl. 487.

Smith's Lark Bunting

Adult Male.

Drawn from Nature by J. J. Audubon, F.R.S. F.L.S.

Lith. Printed & Col^{d} by J. T. Bowen, Philad^{a}

No. 31 Pl. 155.

Snow Lark Bunting

1. 2. Adult. 3. Young.

Drawn from Nature by J. J. Audubon F.R.S. F.L.S.

Lith.d Printed & Col.d by J. T. Bowen, Philada.

No. 100. Pl. 500.

W.A.M.

Baird's Bunting

Male

Drawn from Nature by J. J. Audubon F.R.S. F.L.S.

Lith. Printed & Col.d by J. T. Bowen Philad.a

No. 32 Pl. 159.

R.T.

Bay-winged Bunting.

Male.

Prickly Pear Cactus Opuntia

Drawn from Nature by J. J. Audubon F.R.S.F.L.S. Lith.d Printed & Col.d by J. T. Bowen Philad.a

No. 32. Pl. 156.

R. N.

Black-throated Bunting.

1. Male. 2. Female.

Phalaris arundinacea and Antirrhinum Linaria

Drawn from Nature by J. J. Audubon, F.R.S.F.L.S. Lith.d Printed & Col.d by J. T. Bowen, Philad.a

N°34. Pl.166.

Canada Bunting (Tree Sparrow.)

1. Male. 2. Female.

Canadian Barberry.

Drawn from Nature by J. J. Audubon F.R.S.F.L.S. Lith.d Printed & Col.d by J. T. Bowen Philad.a

No. 33. Pl. 165.

R.T.

Chipping Bunting.

Male.

Black locust or False Acacia.
Robina pseudacacia.

Drawn from Nature by J. J. Audubon F.R.S.F.L.S.

Lith.d Printed & Col.d by J. T. Bowen. Philad.a

R. T.

Clay-coloured Bunting.

Male.

Asclepias tuberosa?

Drawn from Nature by J. J. Audubon F.R.S.F.L.S.

Lith.d Printed & Col.d by J. T. Bowen. Philad.a

R.T.

Field Bunting.

Male.

Calopogon pulchellus. Brown.
Dwarf Huckle-berry. Vaccinium tenellum.

Drawn from Nature by J. J. Audubon F.R.S.F.L.S. Lith.d Printed & Col.d by J. T. Bowen Philad.a

R T

Henslow's Bunting.

Male.

Indian Pink-root or Worm-grass.
Spigelia Marilandica
Phlox aristata.

R. T.

Lark Bunting.

Male.

Drawn from Nature by J. J. Audubon F.R.S. F.L.S.

Lith.d Printed & Col.d by J. T. Bowen Philad.a

No. 98. Pl. 488.

Le Conte's Sharp-tailed Bunting

Male

Drawn from Nature by J. J. Audubon, F.R.S.F.L.S. Lith. Printed & Col.d by J. T. Bowen, Philad.a

R.T.

Savannah Bunting

1. Male. 2. Female.

Indian Pink-root. Spigelia Marilandica.

Drawn from Nature by J.J. Audubon F.R.S.F.L.S.

Lith.d Printed & Col.d by J.T. Bowen, Philada.

W. E. ct.

Shattucks Bunting

Male

Drawn from Nature by J. J. Audubon, F.R.S.F.L.S. Lith. Printed & Col.d by J. T. Bowen, Philad.a

R.T.

Townsend's Bunting.

Male.

Drawn from Nature by J. J. Audubon F.R.S. F.L.S.

Lith.d Printed & Col.d by J. T. Bowen Philad.a

R. T.

Yellow-winged Bunting.

Male.

Drawn from Nature by J. J. Audubon F.R.S.F.L.S.

Lith.d Printed & Col.d by J. T. Bowen Philad.a

R.T.

Common Snow-Bird.

1. Male. 2. Female.

Drawn from Nature by J. J. Audubon. F.R.S. F.L.S.

Lith.d Printed & Col.d by J. T. Bowen, Philad.

R.T.

Oregon Snow Bird

1. Male 2. Female.

Rosa Laevigata

Drawn from Nature by J. J. Audubon F.R.S.F.L.S.

Lith.d Printed & Col.d by J. T. Bowen. Philad.a

Indigo Bunting.

1. 2. 3. Males in different States of Plumage. 4. Female.

Wild Sarsaparilla.

Drawn from Nature by J.J.Audubon, F.R.S.F.L.S. Lith.d Printed & Col.d by J. T. Bowen, Philad.a

R.5

Lazuli Finch.

1. Male 2. Female.

Wild Spanish Coffee.

Drawn from Nature by J. J. Audubon F.R.S.F.L.S.

Lith.d Printed & Col.d by J. T. Bowen. Philad.a

Painted Bunting

1. 2. 3. Males in different States of Plumage. 4. Female.

Chicasaw Wild Plum.

Drawn from Nature by J. J. Audubon F.R.S. F.L.S.

Lith.d Printed & Col.d by J. T. Bowen. Philad.a

No. 35.

Pl 173.

Macgillivray's Shore-Finch.

1. Male 2. Female.

Drawn from Nature by J. J. Audubon, F.R.S.F.L.S.

Lith.d Printed & Col.d by J. T. Bowen, Philad.a

No. 35. Pl. 172.

R.T

Sea-side Finch.

1 Male 2 Female

Carolina Rose.

Drawn from Nature by J. J. Audubon F.R.S.F.L.S.

Lith.d Printed & Col.d by J. T. Bowen. Philad.a

No. 35. Pl. 174.

Sharp-tailed Finch.

1. Males. 2. Female & Nest.

Drawn from Nature by J. J. Audubon F.R.S.F.L.S. Lith.d Printed & Col.d by J. T. Bowen Philad.a

R. T.

Swamp Sparrow

Male.

May-apple

Drawn from Nature by Mrs. Lucy Audubon. Lith. Printed & Col. by J. T. Bowen Philad.

Bachman's Pinewood Finch

Male.

Pinckneya pubescens.

Drawn from Nature by J. J. Audubon F.R.S.F.L.S.   Lith.d Printed & Col.d by J. T. Bowen, Philad.a

Lincoln's Pinewood Finch.

1. Male. 2. Female.

1. Dwarf Cornel. 2. Cloudberry. 3. Glaucous Kalmia.

Drawn from Nature by J. J. Audubon F.R.S. F.L.S. Lith.d Printed & Col.d by J. T. Bowen Philad.

Lesser Redpoll Linnet.

1. Male 2. Female.

Drawn from Nature by J. J. Audubon F.R.S. F.L.S. Lith.d Printed & Col.d by J. T. Bowen Philad.

Mealy Redpoll Linnet.

Male.

Drawn from Nature by J. J. Audubon, F.R.S. F.L.S.

Lith.d Printed & Col.d by J. T. Bowen, Philad.a

Pine Linnet.

1 Male. 2. Female

Black Larch.

Drawn from Nature by J. J. Audubon, F.R.S. F.L.S.

Lith. Printed & Col.d by J. T. Bowen, Philad.

American Goldfinch

1 Male. 2. Female

Common Thistle

Drawn from Nature by J. J. Audubon F.R.S.F.L.S.

Lith.d Printed & Col.d by J. T. Bowen Philad.

Arkansaw Goldfinch.

Male.

Drawn from Nature by J. J. Audubon F.R.S.F.L.S.

Lith.d Printed & Col.d by J. T. Bowen, Philad.

No. 37 Pl. 182.

Black-headed Goldfinch.

Male

Drawn from Nature by J. J. Audubon F.R.S.F.L.S. Lith.d Printed & Col.d by J. T. Bowen, Philad.

Stanley Goldfinch.

Drawn from Nature by J. J. Audubon F.R.S.F.L.S. Lith.d Printed & Col.d by J. T. Bowen Philad.

Yarrell's Goldfinch

1 Male. 2 Female.

Drawn from Nature by J. J. Audubon F.R.S.F.L.S.

Lith.d Printed & Col.d by J. T. Bowen Philad.

No. 39

Pl. 193.

Black-and-yellow-crowned Finch.

Drawn from Nature by J. J. Audubon F.R.S.F.L.S.

Lith.d Printed & Col.d by J. T. Bowen Philad.

Brown Finch

Female

Drawn from Nature by J. J. Audubon, F.R.S. F.L.S. Lith.d Printed & Col.d by J. T. Bowen Philad.a

Pl. 186.
No. 38
Fox-coloured Finch.
1. Male. 2. Female.
Drawn from Nature by J.J.Audubon. F.R.S.F.L.S.
Lith.d Printed & Col.d by J.T. Bowen, Philad.a

No. 97. Pl. 484.

Harris' Finch

1. Adult Male. 2. Young Female.

Drawn from Nature by J. J. Audubon, F.R.S. F.L.S.

Lith. Printed & Col.d by J. T. Bowen, Phila.

Song Finch

1. Male. 2. Female.

Huckle-berry or Blue tangled Vaccinium frondosum?

Drawn from Nature by J.J.Audubon. F.R.S.F.L.S.

Lith.d Printed & Col.d by J.T.Bowen. Philad.a

Morton's Finch.

Male.

Drawn from Nature by J. J. Audubon F.R.S.F.L.S.

Lith.d Printed & Col.d by J. T. Bowen. Philad.

Townsend's Finch

Male.

Drawn from Nature by J. J. Audubon. F.R.S.F.L.S.

Lith.d Printed & Col.d by J. T. Bowen. Philad.a

White-crowned Finch.

1. Male. 2. Female.

Wild Summer Grape.

Drawn from Nature by J.J.Audubon, F.R.S.F.L.S. Lith.d Printed & Col.d by J.T. Bowen, Philad.a

White-throated Finch.

1. Male. 2. Female.

Common Dogwood.

Drawn from Nature by J.J. Audubon, F.R.S.F.L.S. Lith.d Printed & Col.d by J. T. Bowen, Philad.a

Pl. 194.

No. 39

Arctic Ground Finch.

1. Male, 2. Female

Drawn from Nature by J. J. Audubon F.R.S.F.L.S

Lith.d Printed & Col.d by J. T. Bowen, Philad.

No. 39 Pl. 195.

Towhe Ground Finch.

1. Male. 2. Female.

Common Blackberry.

Drawn from Nature by J. J. Audubon F.R.S.F.L.S.

Lith.d Printed & Col.d by J. T. Bowen Philad.

Crimson-fronted Purple Finch.

Male.

Drawn from Nature by J. J. Audubon F.R.S.F.L.S. Lith.d Printed & Col.d by J. T. Bowen Philad.

No. 40. Pl. 196.

Crested Purple Finch.

1. Males. 2. Female

Red Larch. Larix Americana.

Drawn from Nature by J.J. Audubon, F.R.S.F.L.S.

Lith.d Printed & Col.d by J. T. Bowen, Philad.a

No. 40.

Pl. 198.

Grey-crowned Purple Finch.

Male.

Stokesia cyanea.

Drawn from Nature by J. J. Audubon F.R.S.F.L.S.

Lith.d Printed & Col.d by J. T. Bowen Philad.

Nº 40.

Pl. 199

Common Pine-finch

1. Male. 2. Female.

Drawn from Nature by J. J. Audubon. F.R.S.F.L.S.

Lith.d Printed & Col.d by J. T. Bowen Phil.

Common Crossbill.

1. Males. 2. Females.

Drawn from Nature by J. J. Audubon F.R.S.F.L.S. *Lith.d Printed & Col.d by J. T. Bowen Phil.*

No. 41

Pl. 201.

White-winged Crossbill.

1. Males: 2. Female.

Drawn from Nature by J.J.Audubon, F.R.S.F.L.S. Lith.d Printed & Col.d by J. T. Bowen, Philad.a

No. 41. Pl. 202.

Prairie Lark-Finch.

1. Male. 2. Female.

Drawn from Nature by J. J. Audubon F.R.S.F.L.S.

Lith.d Printed & Col.d by J. T. Bowen, Philad.

Common Cardinal Grosbeak.

1. Male. 2. Female.

Wild Almond. Prunus caroliniana.

Drawn from Nature by J. J. Audubon. F.R.S.F.L.S. Lith.d Printed & Col.d by J. T. Bowen. Phil.

Black-headed Song-Grosbeak.

1. Males 2 Female.

Blue Song Grosbeak.

1. Male. 2. Female. 3. Young.

Drawn from Nature by J. J. Audubon, F.R.S.F.L.S. *Lith.d Printed & Col.d by J. T. Bowen, Philad.*

Rose-breasted Song-Grosbeak.

1. Males. 2. Female. 3. Young Male.

Ground Hemlock Taxus canadensis.

Drawn from Nature by J.J. Audubon, F.R.S.F.L.S.

Lith.d Printed & Col.d by J. T. Bowen, Philad.a

No. 42. Pl. 207.

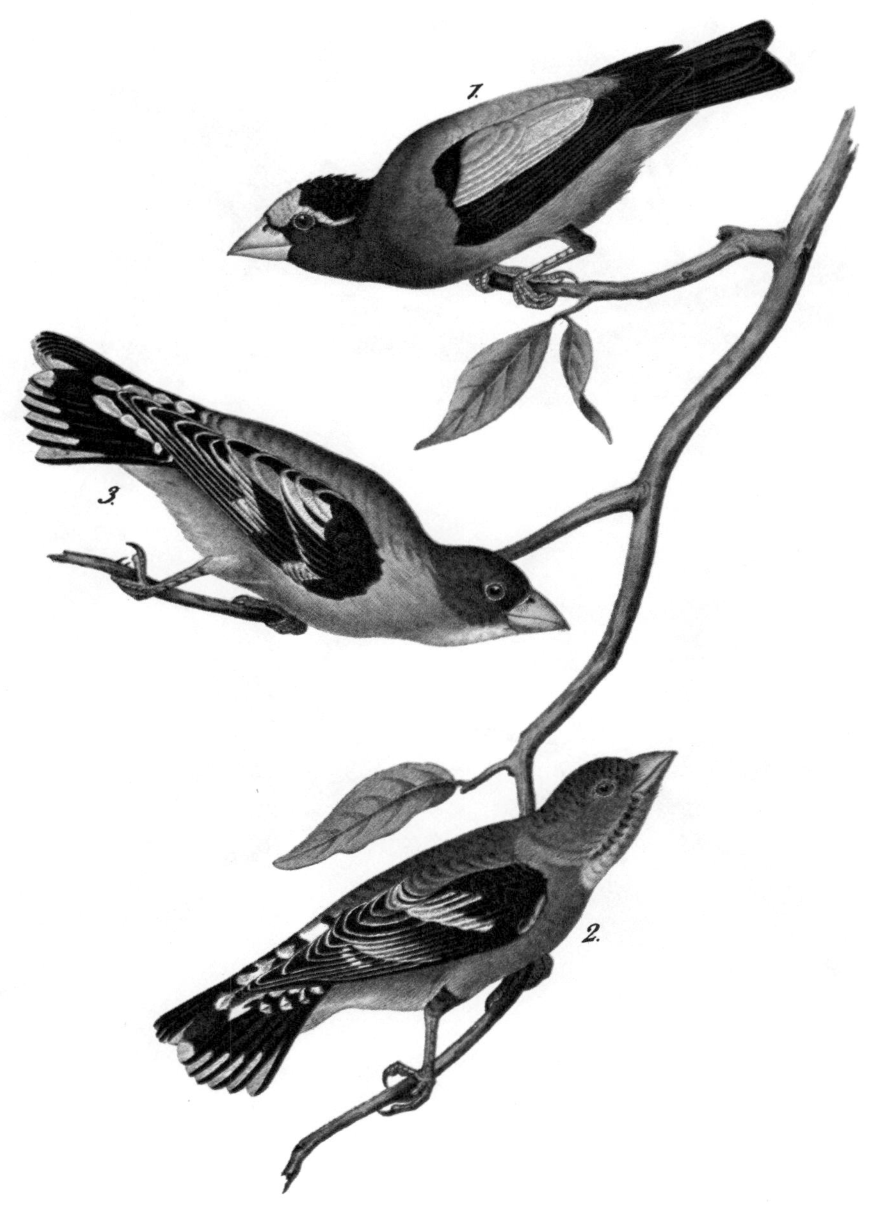

Evening Grosbeak.

1. Male 2. Female 3 Young Male

Drawn from Nature by J. J. Audubon. F.R.S.F.L.S. Lith.d Printed & Col.d by J. T. Bowen-Philad.

Louisiana Tanager.

1. Males. 2. Female.

Drawn from Nature by J.J.Audubon, F.R.S.F.L.S.

Lith. Printed & Col. by J. T. Bowen, Philad.

Scarlet Tanager.

1. Male. 2. Female.

Drawn from Nature by J. J. Audubon. F.R.S.F.L.S.   Lith.d Printed & Col.d by J. T. Bowen, Philad.

Summer Red-bird

1. Male. 2. Female. 3. Young Male.

Wild Muscadine Vitis rotundifolia. Mich

Drawn from Nature by J.J. Audubon, F.R.S.F.L.S.

Lith.d Printed & Col.d by J. T. Bowen, Philad.a

No. 43.
Pl. 211.
1.
2.
Wandering Rice-bird.
1 Male. 2 Female
Red Maple. Acer Rubrum.
Drawn from Nature by J. J. Audubon. F.R.S.F.L.S.
Lith.d Printed & Col.d by J. T. Bowen Philad.

Nº 43.
Pl. 212.
1.
2.
3.
Common Cow-bird.
1. Male. 2 Female. 3 Young.
Drawn from Nature by J.J. Audubon, F.R.S.F.L.S.
Lith.d Printed & Col.d by J.T. Bowen, Philad.

N°. 43. Pl. 215.

Red-and-black-shouldered Marsh-Blackbird

1. Male 2. Female.

Drawn from Nature by J. J. Audubon F.R.S.F.L.S.

Lith.ᵈ Printed & Col.ᵈ by J. T. Bowen Philad.

No. 43. Pl. 214.

Red-and-white-shouldered Marsh Blackbird

Male.

Drawn from Nature by J. J. Audubon F.R.S.F.L.S.

Lith.d Printed & Col.d by J. T. Bowen Philad.

Red-winged Starling

1 Male Adult. 2. Young Male. 3 Female.

Red Maple

Drawn from Nature by J. J. Audubon F.R.S.F.L.S. Lith.d Printed & Col.d by J. T. Bowen. Philad.

Saffron-headed Marsh-Blackbird.

1. Male. 2. Female 3. Young Male.

Drawn from Nature by J. J. Audubon F.R.S.F.L.S.

Lith.d Printed & Col.d by J. T. Bowen, Philad.

Baltimore Oriole, or Hang-nest

1 Male adult. 2 Young Male. 3 Female.

Tulip Tree.

Drawn from Nature by J. J. Audubon F.R.S.F.L.S.

Lith.d Printed & Col.d by J. T. Bowen Phil.

No 44.
Pl 218.
2.
3
1.
Bullock's Troopial
1. Male Adult. 2 Young Male 3 Female
Caprifolium flavum.
Drawn from Nature by J. J. Audubon. F.R.S.F.L.S.
Lith.d Printed & Col.d by J. T. Bowen. Phil.

No 100.

Pl 499.

Common Troupial.

Male.

Drawn from Nature by J.J. Audubon, F.R.S.F.L.S.

Lith.d Printed & Col.d by J. T. Bowen, Philad.a

Orchard Oriole or Hang-nest.

1. Male adult. 2. Young Male. 3. Female & Nest.

Honey Locust.

Drawn from Nature by J. J. Audubon, F.R.S.F.L.S.

Lithd Printed & Cold b, T Bowen, Phil.

N°44. Pl. 220.

Boat-tailed Grackle.

1. Male. 2. Female.

Live Oak.

Drawn from Nature by J.J.Audubon. F.R.S.F.L.S.

Lith.d Printed & Col.d by J. T. Bowen. Phil.

No. 99

Pl. 492.

R.T.

Brewers Black-bird.

Drawn from Nature by J. J. Audubon F.R.S.F.L.S.

Male

Lith. Printed & Col.d by J. T. Bowen, Philad.a

No. 45. Pl. 221.

Common, or Purple Crow-Blackbird.

1. Male. 2. Female.

Maize or Indian Corn.

Drawn from Nature by J. J. Audubon F.R.S.F.L.S. Lith.d Printed & Col.d by J. T. Bowen Philad.

No. 45. Pl 222.

Rusty Crow-Blackbird.

1. Male. 2 Female. 3 Young.

Black Haw.

Lith^d Printed & Col^d by J. T. Bowen Philad.

Meadow Starling or Meadow Lark.

1. Males. 2. Female and Nest.

Yellow flowered Gerardia.

Drawn from Nature by J.J. Audubon, F.R.S.F.L.S.

Lith.d Printed & Col.d by J. T. Bowen, Philad.a

Missouri Meadow Lark.

Male

Drawn from Nature by J.J. Audubon, F.R.S. F.L.S.

Lith. Printed & Col.d by J.T. Bowen, Philad.a

No. 45. Pl. 225.

Common American Crow

Male.

Black Walnut

Drawn from Nature by J. J. Audubon. F.R.S.F.L.S. *Lith.d Printed & Col.d by J. T. Bowen. Phil.*

Fish Crow.

1 Male. 2 Female.

Honey Locust.

Drawn from Nature by J. J. Audubon F.R.S.F.L.S. Lith.d Printed & Col.d by J. T. Bowen Phil.

Nº 45. Pl. 224.

Raven

Old Male.

Thick-Shell bark Hickory.

Drawn from Nature by J. J. Audubon F.R.S. F.L.S. Lith.ᵈ Printed & Colᵈ by J. T. Bowen Philad.

No. 46. Pl. 229.

Columbia Magpie or Jay.

Males

Drawn from Nature by J. J. Audubon F.R.S.F.L.S. Lith.d Printed & Col.d by J. T. Bowen Phil.

No. 46. Pl. 227

Common Magpie.

1. Male 2. Female.

Drawn from Nature by J. J. Audubon. F.R.S.F.L.S. *Lith.d Printed & Col.d by J. T. Bowen. Philad.*

N°. 46

Pl. 228.

Yellow-billed Magpie.

Male.

Plantanus.

Drawn from Nature by J. J. Audubon F.R.S.F.L.S.

Lith.d Printed & Col.d by J. T. Bowen Philad.

No. 47. Pl. 231.

Blue Jay

1. Male. 2 & 3. Female

Trumpet flower. Bignonia radicans.

Drawn from Nature by J. J. Audubon. F.R.S. F.L.S. Lith.d Printed & Col.d by J. T. Bowen. Philad.

N°. 47.
Pl. 234
1.
2.
3.
Canada Jay
1. Male. 2. Female. 3. Young
White Oak. Quercus alba.
Drawn from Nature by J. J. Audubon. F.R.S.F.L.S.
Lith.d Printed & Col.d by J. T. Bowen. Phil.

R. 3.

Florida Jay

1. Male. 2. Female.

Persimontree. Diospyros Virginiana.

Drawn from Nature by J. J. Audubon. F.R.S. F.L.S. Lith.d Printed & Col.d by J. T. Bowen. Phil.

R.T.

Stellers Jay

Male.

Drawn from Nature by J. J. Audubon F.R.S.F.L.S.

Lith.d Printed & Col.d by J. T. Bowen, Phil.a

No. 47. Pl. 232.

Ultramarine Jay

Adult Male.

Drawn from Nature by J. J. Audubon F.R.S. F.L.S. *Lith.d Printed & Col.d by J. T. Bowen Phil.*

No. 47. Pl. 235.

Clarke's Nutcracker.

1. Male. 2. Female.

Drawn from Nature by J. J. Audubon, F.R.S. F.L.S.

Lith. Printed & Col. by J. T. Bowen, Philad.

Great American Shrike.

1. Male. 2. Female. 3. Young.

Cratægus Apiifolia.

Drawn from Nature by J. J. Audub... F.R.S.F.L.S

Lith.d Printed & Col.d by J. T. Bowen. Phil.

R.T.

Loggerhead Shrike

1. Male. 2. Female.

Greenbriar or Round-leaved Smilax. Smilax Rotundifolia

Drawn from Nature by J. J. Audubon, F.R.S. F.L.S. Lith. Printed & Col. by J. T. Bowen, Philad.

Bartrams Vireo or Greenlet

Male

Ipomea

Drawn from Nature by J. J. Audubon. F.R.S.F.L.S. Lith.d Printed & Col.d by J. T. Bowen. Phil.

No. 97. Pl. 485.

Bell's Vireo.

Male.

Rattle-snake Root

Drawn from Nature by J. J. Audubon, F.R.S.F.L.S. Lith. Printed & Col^d by J. T. Bowen, Phila.

No. 49. Pl. 243.

Red-eyed Vireo or Greenlet.

Male.

Honey - locust.

Drawn from Nature by J. J. Audubon F.R.S. F.L.S. Lith.d Printed & Col.d by J. T. Bowen. Phil.

No. 48. Pl. 239.

Solitary Vireo or Greenlet.

1. Male. 2. Female.

American Cane. Miegia macrosperma.

Drawn from Nature by J. J. Audubon F.R.S.F.L.S. Lith.d Printed & Col.d by J. T. Bowen, Phil.

No. 49. Pl. 241.

Warbling Vireo or Greenlet

1. Male. 2. Female.

Swamp Magnolia

Drawn from Nature by J. J. Audubon, F.R.S. F.L.S. Lith.d Printed & Col.d by J. T. Bowen, Philad.

White-eyed Vireo, or Greenlet.

Male.

Pride of China, or bead tree. Melia Azedarach.

Drawn from Nature by J. J. Audubon. F.R.S.F.L.S.   Lith.d Printed & Col.d by J. T. Bowen, Phil.

R.T.

Yellow-throated Vireo, or Greenlet.

Male.

Swamp Snowball. Hydrangea quercifolia.

Drawn from Nature by J. J. Audubon F.R.S. F.L.S. Lith^d. Printed & Col^d. by J. T. Bowen, Philad.

No. 49. Pl. 244.

Yellow-breasted Chat

1. 2. 3. Male 4. Female.
Sweet briar.

Drawn from Nature by J. J. Audubon, F.R.S. F.L.S. Lith.d Printed & Col.d by J. T. Bowen, Phil.

N° 49. Pl. 245.

Black throated Wax-wing. or Bohemian Chatterer.

1. Male. 2. Female.

Canadian Service Tree.

Drawn from Nature by J. J. Audubon F.R.S. F.L.S. Lith.d Printed & Col.d by J. T. Bowen, Philad.

Cedar bird, or Cedar Wax-wing

1. Male 2. Female.

Red Cedar.

Drawn from Nature by J. J. Audubon. F.R.S. F.L.S.

Lith^d Printed & Col^d by J. T. Bowen. Philad.

Brown-headed Nuthatch

1. Male. 2. Female.

Drawn from Nature by J. J. Audubon F.R.S. F.L.S. Lith.d Printed & Col.d by J. T. Bowen. Phil.

Californian Nuthatch.

Adults.

Drawn from Nature by J. J. Audubon F.R.S.F.L.S. Lith.d Printed & Col.d by J. T. Bowen Phil.

Red-bellied Nuthatch

1. Male 2. Female.

Drawn from Nature by J. J. Audubon, F.R.S.F.L.S. *Lith.d Printed & Col.d by J. T. Bowen, Phil.*

No. 50. PL 247.

White-breasted Nuthatch.

1. Male. 2 & 3. Female

Drawn from Nature by J. J. Audubon. F.R.S.F.L.S. *Lith.d Printed & Col.d by J. T. Bowen. Phil.*

Anna Humming bird.

1. 2. Males. 3 Female.

Hibiscus Virginicus.

Drawn from Nature by J.J. Audubon, F.R.S.F.L.S. Lith.d Printed & Col.d by J. T. Bowen, Philad.a

Mango Humming bird

1. 2. Males. 3. Female

Bignonia grandifolia.

Drawn from Nature by J. J. Audubon. F.R.S.F.L.S. Lith.d Printed & Col.d by J. T. Bowen. Phil.

N°. 51. Pl. 253.

Ruby-throated Humming bird

1. 2. Males. 3. Female. — 4 Young

(*Bignonia - radicans*

Drawn from Nature by J.J. Audubon F.R.S.F.L.S. Lith.d Printed & Col.d by J.T. Bowen. Phil.a

No. 51. Pl. 254.

Ruff-necked Humming bird.

1. 2. Males. 3. Female.

Cleome heptaphylla.

Drawn from Nature by J. J. Audubon F.R.S.F.L.S. Lith.d Printed & Col.d by J. T. Bowen. Phil.

No. 51. Pl. 255.

W. H.

Belted Kingfisher

Alcedo Alcyon.

1. Males 2. Female

Drawn from Nature by J. J. Audubon, F.R.S.F.L.S. *Lith.d Printed & Col.d by J. T. Bowen, Phil.*

No. 54. Pl. 268.

Arctic three-toed Woodpecker.

1. 2. Males. 3. Female.

Drawn from Nature by J. J. Audubon. F.R.S.F.L.S.

Lith.d Printed & Col.d by J. T. Bowen. Phil.

A. V.

Audubons' Woodpecker.

Male.

Drawn from Nature by J. J. Audubon F.R.S.F.L.S. Lith.d Printed & Col.d by J. T. Bowen, Phil.

Banded three-toed Woodpecker.

1. Male 2. Female.

Drawn from Nature by J. J. Audubon. F.R.S.F.L.S.

Nº 52.

Canadian Woodpecker.

Male.

Drawn from Nature by J. J. Audubon F.R.S.F.L.S

Lith.d Printed & Col.d by J. T. Bowen, Phil.

No. 53.
Pl. 263.
1.
2.
J.G.
Downy Woodpecker
1. Male. 2. Female
Drawn from Nature by J. J. Audubon F.R.S. F.L.S.
Lith.d Printed & Col.d by J. T. Bowen, Phil.

No. 55.

Pl. 273.

Golden-winged Woodpecker

1. Male. 2. Females.

Drawn from Nature by J.J. Audubon F.R.S.F.L.S.

Lith.d Printed & Col.d by J.T. Bowen Phil.

No. 53. Pl. 262.

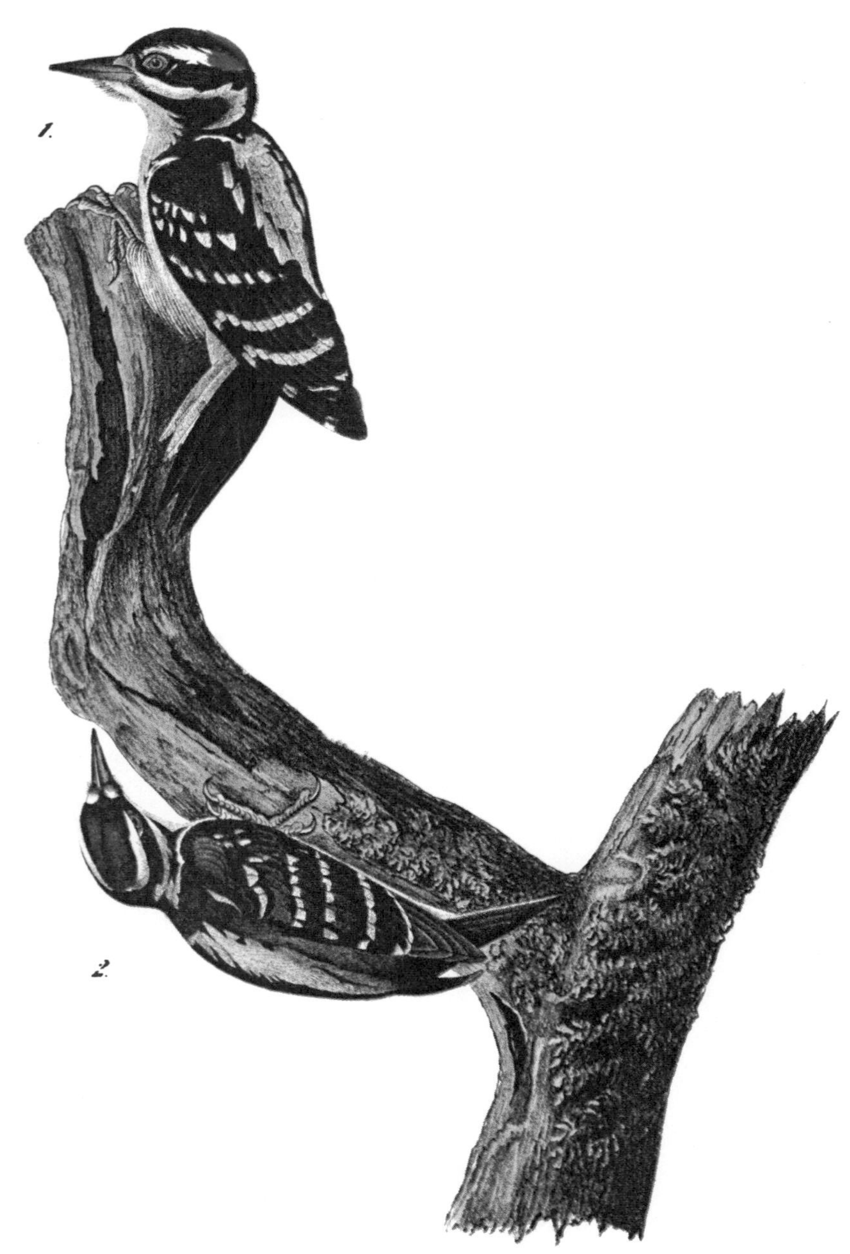

Hairy Woodpecker.

1. Male 2. Female

Drawn from Nature by J. J. Audubon F.R.S. F.L.S. Lith.d Printed & Col.d by J. T. Bowen Phil.

No. 53. Pl. 261.

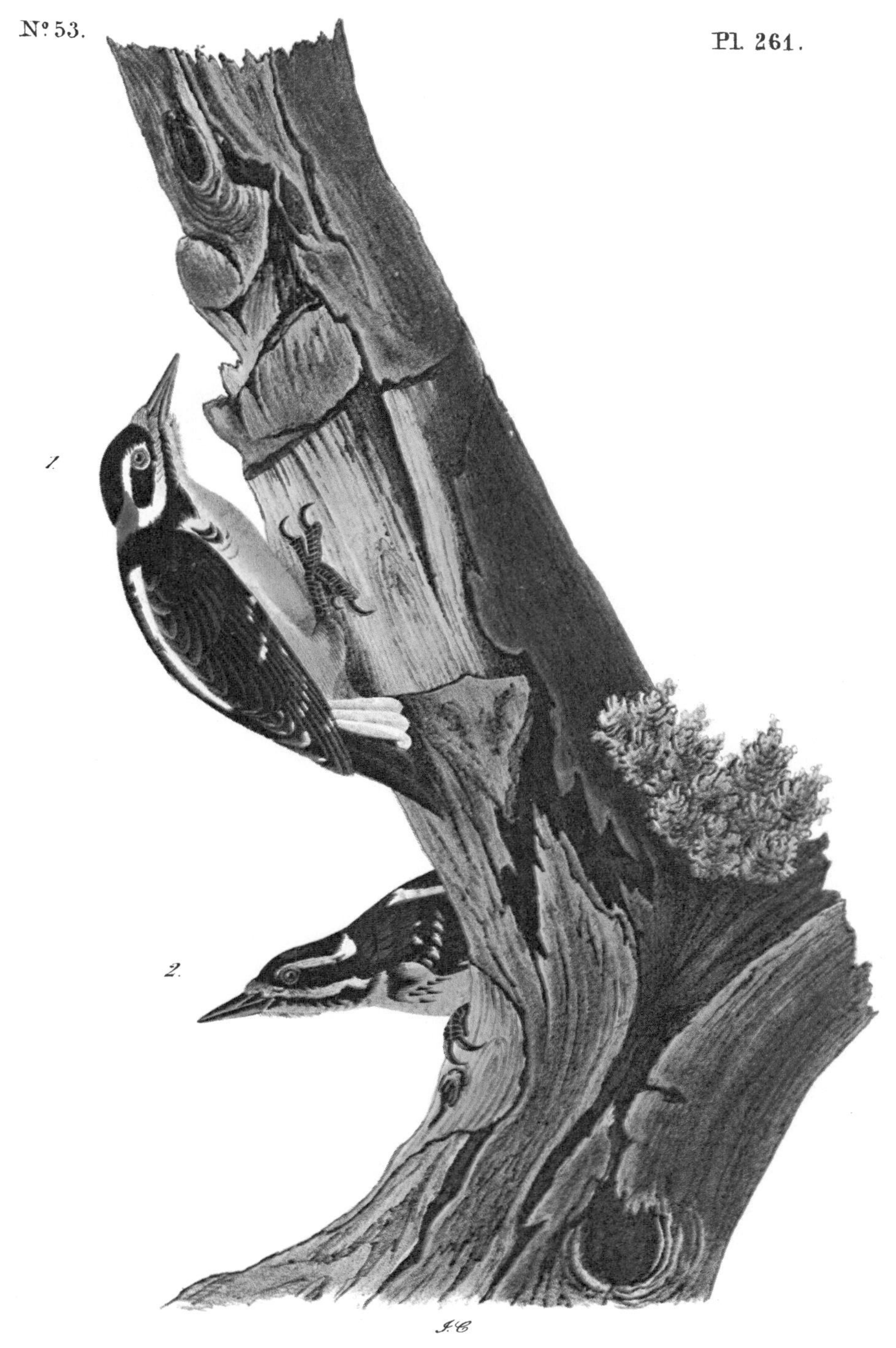

Harris's Woodpecker

1. Male. 2. Female.

Drawn from Nature by J. J. Audubon, F.R.S.F.L.S. Lith.d Printed & Col.d by J. T. Bowen, Phil.

No. 52. Pl. 256.

Ivory-billed Woodpecker.

1. Male. 2 & 3. Female.

Drawn from Nature by J. J. Audubon F.R.S.F.L.S. Lithd. Printed & Cold. by J. T. Bowen. Phil.

Lewis' Woodpecker.

Drawn from Nature by J.J.Audubon.F.R.S.F.L.S. 1. Male 2. Female Lith.d Printed & Col.d by J.T.Bowen Phil.

No. 52. Pl. 260.

Maria's Woodpecker.

1. Male. 2. Female.

Drawn from Nature by J. J. Audubon, F.R.S.F.L.S. *Lith.d Printed & Col.d by J. T. Bowen, Phil.*

W.E.H.

Missouri Red-moustached Woodpecker

Male

Drawn from Nature by J. J. Audubon, F.R.S. F.L.S.

Lith. Printed & Col.d by J. T. Bowen, Philad.a

No. 52. Pl. 259.

Phillips' Woodpecker.

Males.

Drawn from Nature by J. J. Audubon, F.R.S.F.L.S. *Lith.d Printed & Col.d by J. T. Bowen, Phil.*

No. 52. Pl. 257.

Pileated Woodpecker

1. Adult Male. 2. Adult Female. 3 and 4. Young Males.

Raccoon Grape.

Drawn from Nature by J. J. Audubon, F.R.S.F.L.S. *Lith.d Printed & Col.d by J. T. Bowen, Phil.*

Red-bellied Woodpecker.

1. Male. 2. Female.

Drawn from Nature by J. J. Audubon, F.R.S.F.L.S. Lith.d Printed & Col.d by J. T. Bowen, Phil.

No. 54.

Pl. 266.

Red-breasted Woodpecker.

1. Male. 2. Female.

Drawn from Nature by J. J. Audubon. F.R.S.F.L.S.

Lith.d Printed & Col.d by J. T. Bowen. Phil.

Red-cockaded Woodpecker.

1. 2. Males 3. Female.

Drawn from Nature by J. J. Audubon F.R.S.F.L.S.

Lith.d Printed & Col.d by J. T. Bowen, Phil.

No. 55. Pl. 271.

Red-headed Woodpecker.

1. Male. 2. Female. 3 Young.

Drawn from Nature by J.J. Audubon, F.R.S.F.L.S.

Lith.d Printed & Col.d by J. T. Bowen, Philad.a

No. 55 Pl. 274.

A.V.

Red-shafted Woodpecker.

1. Male. 2. Female.

Drawn from Nature by J. J. Audubon F.R.S.F.L.S.

Lith.d Printed & Col.d by J. T. Bowen, Phil.

A. C.

Yellow-bellied Woodpecker.

1. Male. 2. Female.

Prunus Caroliniana.

Drawn from Nature by J. J. Audubon, F.R.S. F.L.S. *Lith.d Printed & Col.d by J. T. Bowen, Phil.*

No. 56

Pl. 276

Black-billed Cuckoo.

1. Male 2. Female.

Magnolia grandiflora.

Drawn from Nature by J. J. Audubon F.R.S. F.L.S.

Lith.d Printed & Col.d by J. T. Bowen, Phil.

No. 56.

Pl. 277.

Mangrove Cuckoo.

Male.

Seven years apple.

Drawn from Nature by J.J. Audubon, F.R.S. F.L.S.

Lith.d Printed & Col.d by J.T. Bowen, Phil.

N°. 55
Pl. 275.
2.
1.
W. H.
Yellow-billed Cuckoo
1. Male 2. Female.
Papaw Tree.
Drawn from Nature by J. J. Audubon, F.R.S.F.L.S.
Lith^d. Printed & Col^d. by J. T. Bowen, Phil.

No. 56. Pl. 278.

Carolina Parrot or Parrakeet

1. 2. Males. 3. Female. 4. Young.

Cockle bur.

Drawn from Nature by J. J. Audubon F.R.S.F.L.S. *Lith. Printed & Col.d by J. T. Bowen, Phil.*

Band-tailed Dove or Pigeon.

1. Male. 2. Female.

Cornus nuttallii.

Drawn from Nature by J. J. Audubon F.R.S.F.L.S. Lith^d Printed & Col^d by J. T. Bowen, Phil.

No. 57.

Pl. 284.

Blue-headed Ground Dove or Pigeon

1. Male. 2. Females.

Drawn from Nature by J.J. Audubon, F.R.S. F.L.S.

Lith. Printed & Col. by J.T. Bowen, Phil.

No. 57. Pl. 283.

Ground Dove.

1. & 2. Males. 3. Female. 4. Young

Wild Orange.

Drawn from Nature by J. J. Audubon F.R.S.F.L.S.

Lith.d Printed & Col.d by J. T. Bowen, Phil.

N°. 57. Pl. 282.

Key-West Dove

1. Male. 2. Female.

Drawn from Nature by J. J. Audubon, F.R.S.F.L.S.

Lith.d Printed & Col.d by J. T. Bowen, Philad.

No. 100. Pl. 496.

The Texan Turtle Dove.

Male.

Drawn from Nature by J. J. Audubon, F.R.S. F.L.S. Lith. Printed & Col.d by J. T. Bowen, Philad.a

A. V.

White-headed Dove, or Pigeon

1. Male. 2. Female.

Cordia sebestina.

Drawn from Nature by J. J. Audubon F.R.S.F.L.S. Lith.d Printed & Col.d by J. T. Bowen. Phil.

No. 57. Pl. 281.

W. H.

Zenaida Dove.

1. Male. 2. Female

Anona.

Drawn from Nature by J. J. Audubon. F.R.S.F.L.S.

Lith.d Printed & Col.d by J. T. Bowen. Philad.

No. 57. Pl. 285.

Passenger Pigeon

1. Male 2. Female.

Drawn from Nature by J. J. Audubon F.R.S.F.L.S.

Lith.d Printed & Col.d by J. T. Bowen Phil.

Carolina Turtle Dove.

1. Males 2. Females.

White flowered Stuartia. Stuartia Malacodendron.

Drawn from Nature by J. J. Audubon, F.R.S.F.L.S. Lith.d Printed & Col.d by J. T. Bowen, Philad.a

Wild Turkey.

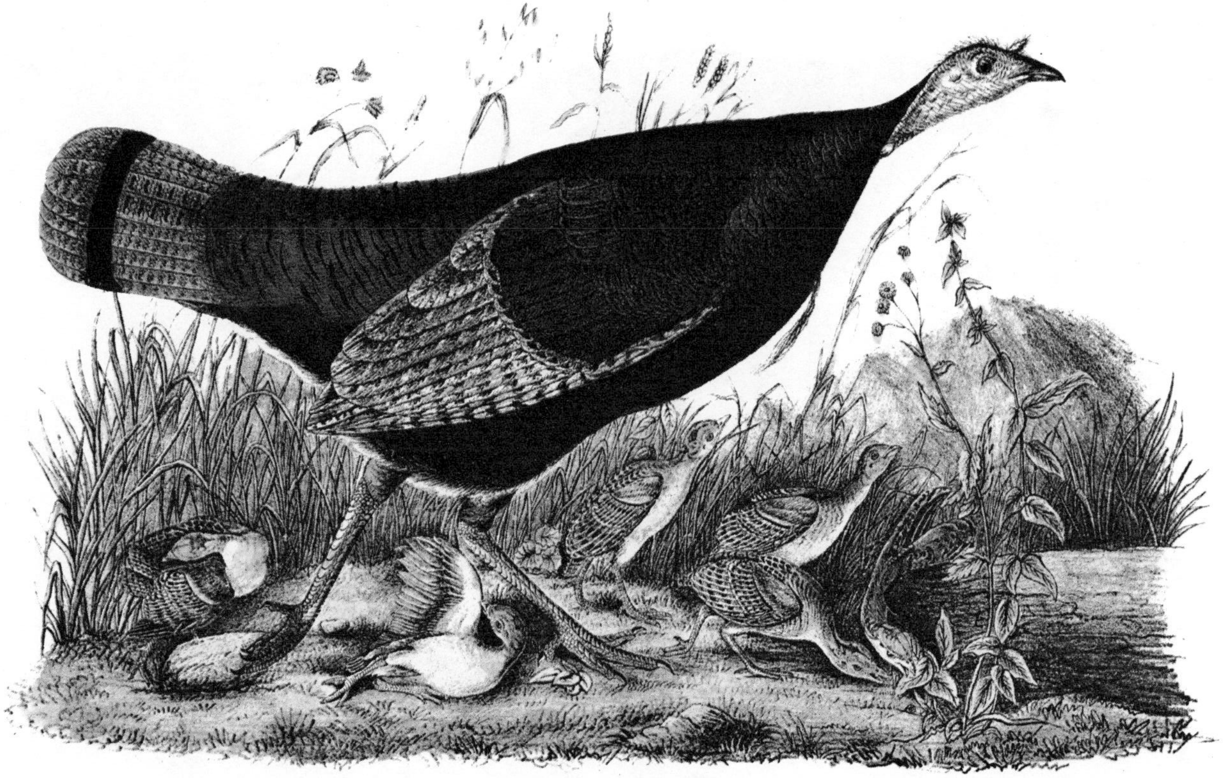

Drawn from Nature by J.J.Audubon, F.R.S.F.L.S. Female & Young. Lith.d Printed & Col.d by J. T. Bowen, Philad.a

J. C.
Wild Turkey
Male.

Drawn from Nature by J. J. Audubon, F.R.S.F.L.S. *Lith^d Printed & Col^d by J. T. Bowen, Phil.*

1. 3. 2.

Common American Partridge.

Drawn from Nature by J.J. Audubon, F.R.S.F.L.S. 1. Male. 2. Female. 3. Young. Lith.d Printed & Col.d by J. T. Bowen, Philad.

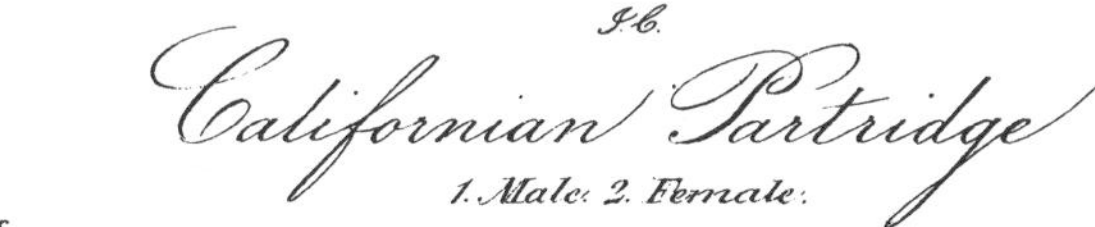

J.C.

Californian Partridge

1. Male. 2. Female.

Drawn from Nature by J. J. Audubon, F.R.S. F.L.S.

Lith.d Printed & Col.d by J. T. Bowen, Phil.

N°. 59.

Pl. 291.

Drawn from Nature by J.J.Audubon, F.R.S.F.L.S.

Plumed Partridge.

1. Male. 2. Female.

No. 59. Pl. 292.

J. C.

Welcome Partridge

Young

Drawn from Nature by J. J. Audubon F.R.S.F.L.S. Lith. Printed & Col.d by J. T. Bowen, Phil.

No. 59.
Pl. 294.
1. 2. 3. 3. 4.
Canada Grouse.
1. 2. Males. 3. Females.
4. Trillium pictum. 5 Streptopus distortus.
Drawn from Nature by J. J. Audubon F.R.S. F.L.S.
Lith.d Printed & Col.d by J. T. Bowen, Phil.

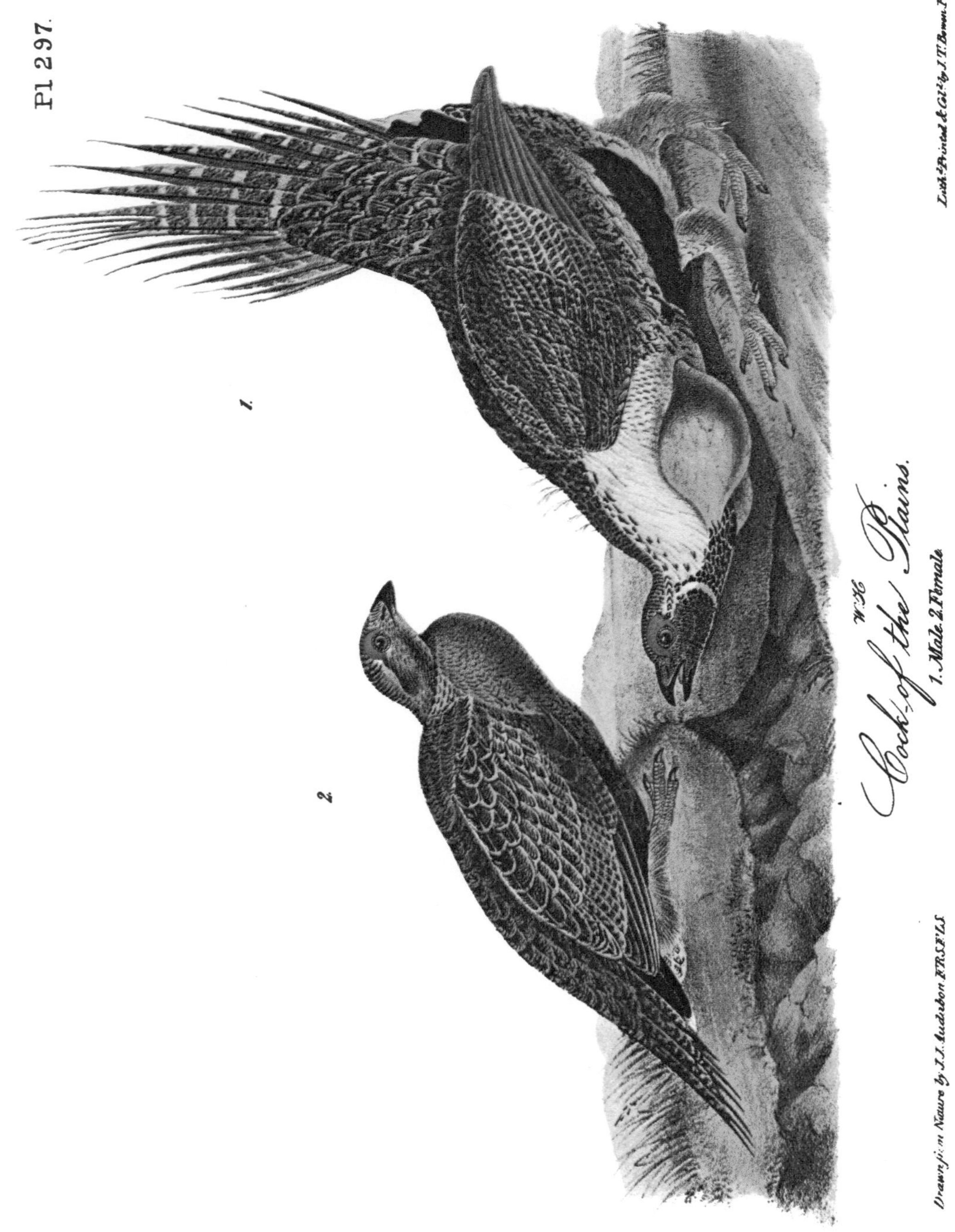
Pl 297.
1
2
W.H.
Cock-of the Plains.
1. Male. 2. Female
Drawn from Nature by J.J. Audubon F.R.S.F.L.S.
Lith.d Printed & Col.d by J.T. Bowen, Phil.

N°. 60.

Pl. 295.
N° 59.
1.
2.
Dusky Grouse.
1. Male. 2. Female
Drawn from Nature by J.J.Audubon F.R.S.F.L.S.
Lith.d Printed & Col.d by J.T. Bowen Philad.

No. 60. Pl. 296.

1 2.

Pinnated Grouse.

1. 2. Males. 3 Female. Lilium Superbum.

Drawn from Nature by J.J. Audubon, F.R.S.F.L.S.

Lith.d Printed & Col.d by J. T. Bowen, Philad.a

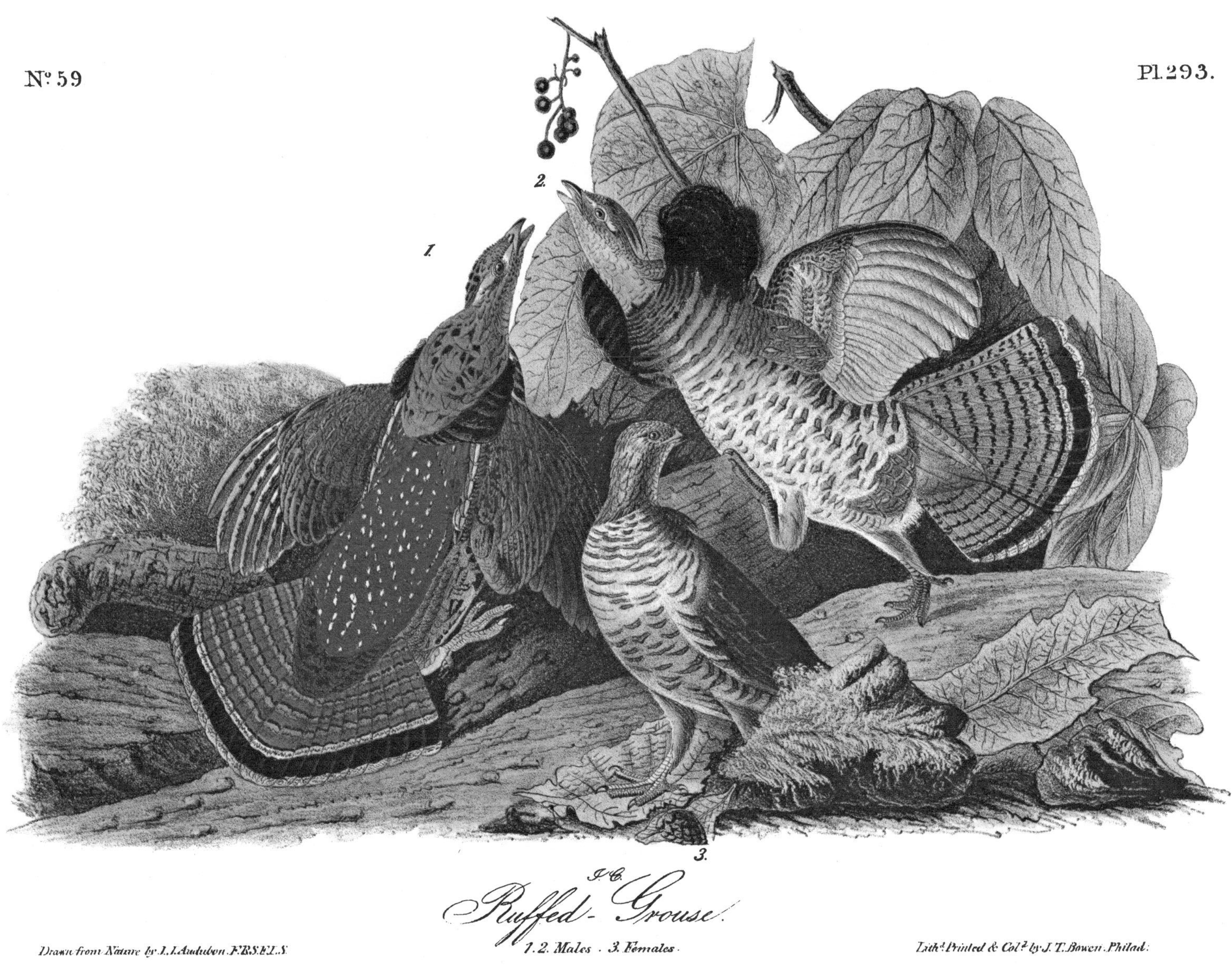

No. 59
Pl.293.
1
2
3
Ruffed Grouse.
1.2. Males. 3. Females.
Drawn from Nature by J.J. Audubon F.R.S.F.L.S.
Lith.d Printed & Col.d by J.T. Bowen, Philad.

No. 60. Pl. 298.

2.

1.

W.H.

Sharp-tailed Grouse.

1. Male. 2. Female.

Drawn from Nature by J.J. Audubon F.R.S.F.L.S.

Lith.d Printed & Col.d by J.T. Bowen, Phil.

No. 60. Pl 300.

American Ptarmigan. [J.G. above Ptarmigan]

Male.

Drawn from Nature by J. J. Audubon F.R.S.F.L.S.

Lith.d Printed & Col.d by J. T. Bowen, Phil.a

No. 61. 2. 1. Pl. 301.

3.

Rock W.H. Ptarmigan

1. Male, in Winter. 2. Female, Summer Plumage. 3. Young in August.

Drawn from Nature by J.J. Audubon F.R.S.F.L.S.

Lith.d Printed & Col.d by J.T. Bowen, Philad.

No. 61

Pl. 302.

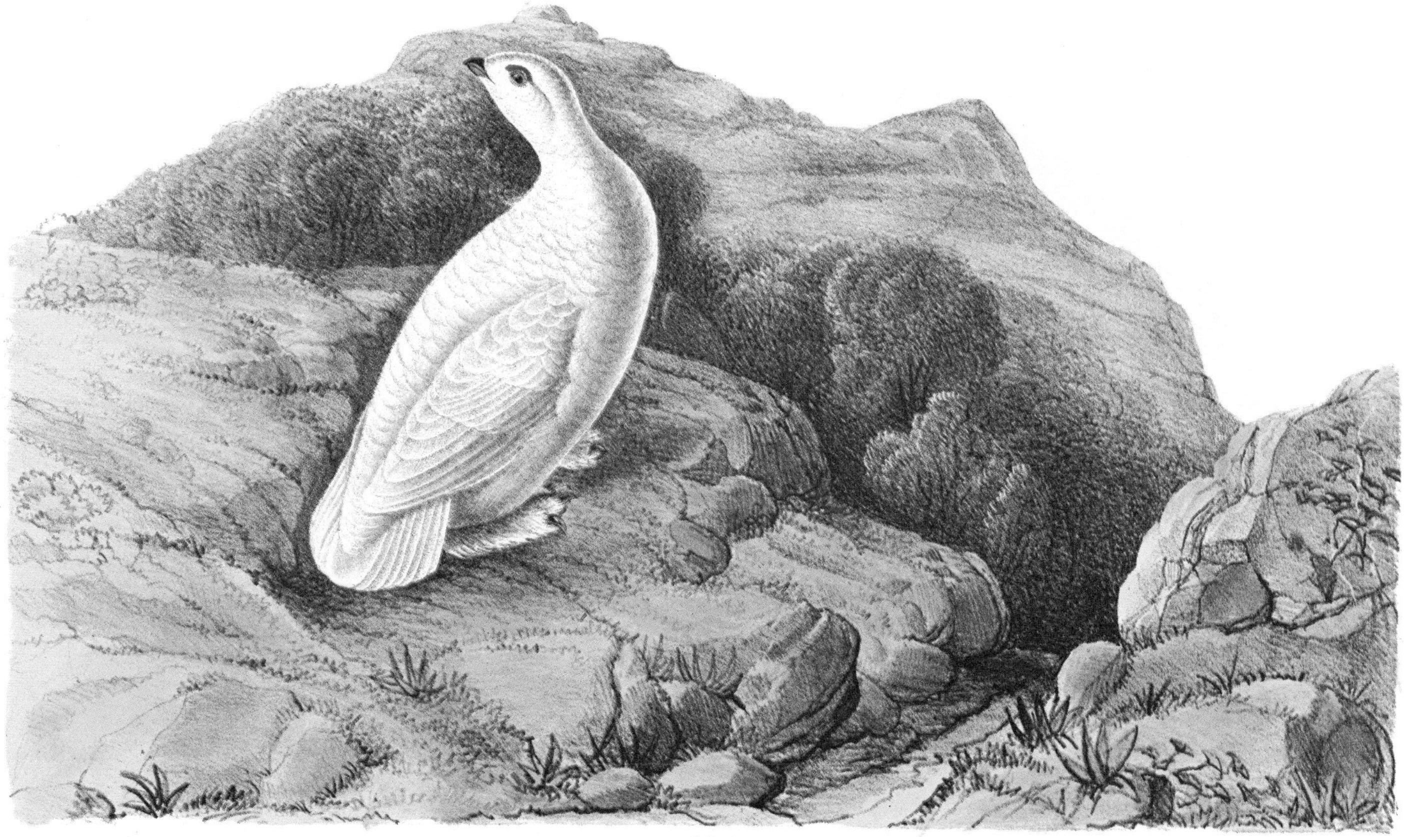

J.C. White-tailed Ptarmigan

Adult, in Winter Plumage

Drawn from Nature by J. J. Audubon F.R.S.F.L.S

Lith.d Printed & Col.d by J. T. Bowen, Philad.

No. 60.

Pl. 299.

Willow Ptarmigan.

1. Male. 2. Female & young

Drawn from Nature by J. J. Audubon F.R.S.F.L.S.

Lith. Printed & Col. by J. T. Bowen Phil.

No. 61.

Pl. 304.

W. H.

Common Gallinule.

Adult Male.

Drawn from Nature by J. J. Audubon, F.R.S.F.L.S.

Lith.d Printed & Col.d by J. T. Bowen, Philad.a

No. 61. Pl. 303.

Purple Gallinule.
Adult Male. Spring Plumage

Drawn from Nature by J. J. Audubon, F.R.S.F.L.S.
Lith.d Printed & Col.d by J. T. Bowen, Phil.

No. 61. Pl. 305.

M. C.

American Coot.

Drawn from Nature by J. J. Audubon, F.R.S.F.L.S.

Lith. Printed & Col. by J. T. Bowen, Philad.

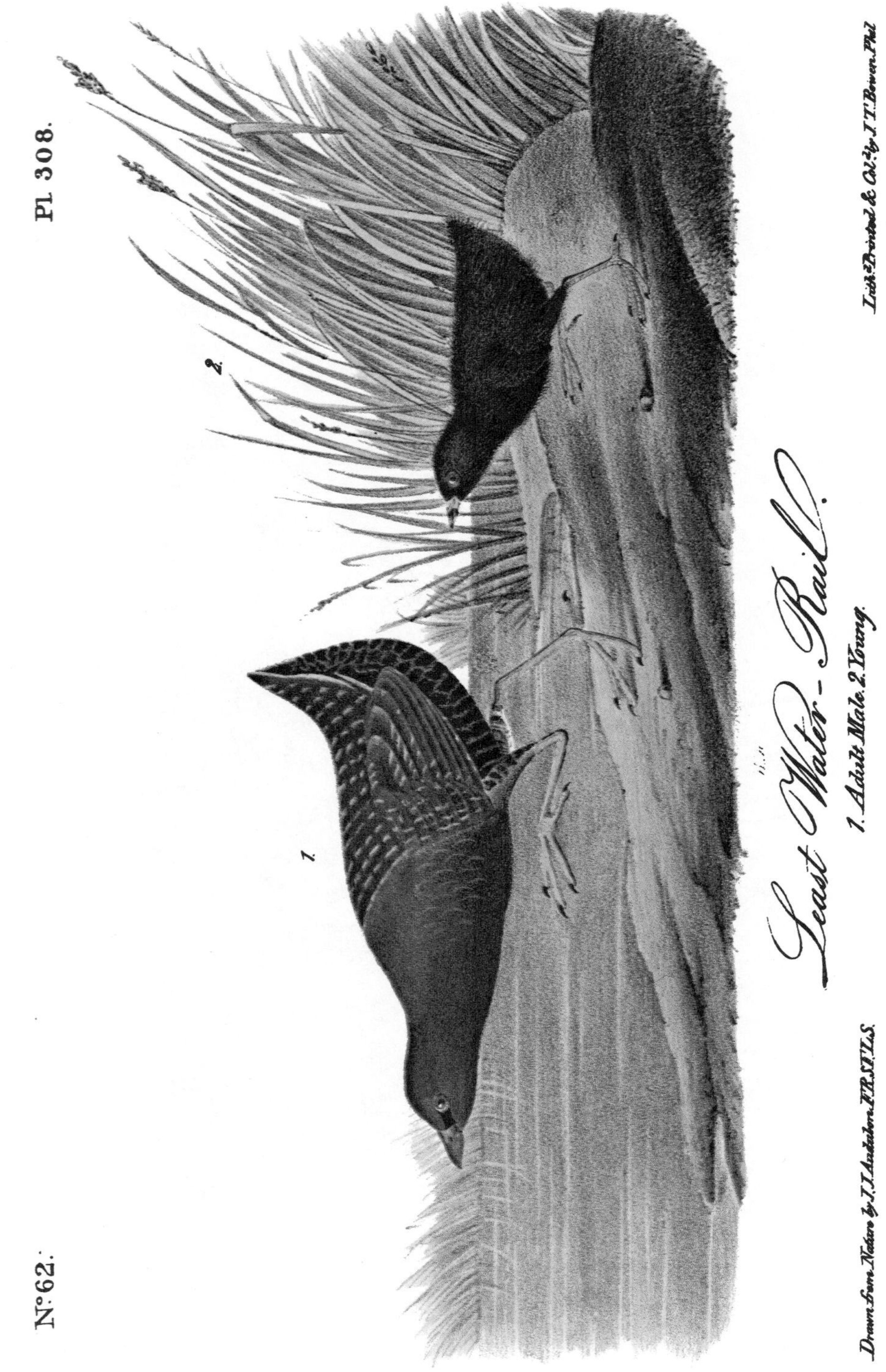
Nº 62.
Pl. 308.
1
2
Least Water-Rail.
1. Adult Male. 2. Young
Drawn from Nature by J.J. Audubon, F.R.S.F.L.S.
Lith.d Printed & Col.d by J.T. Bowen, Phila

No. 62.

Pl. 306.

2.

1.

3.

Sora Rail.

1. Male. — 2. Female. 3. Young.

Drawn from Nature by J. J. Audubon, F.R.S. F.L.S.

Lith. Printed & Col.d by J. T. Bowen, Philada.

No. 62. Pl. 307.

Drawn from Nature by J. J. Audubon F.R.S. F.L.S.

Yellow-breasted Rail.

Adult Male in Spring

Lith.d Printed & Col.d by J. T. Bowen, Phil.

No. 62. Pl. 310.

Clapper Rail or Salt Water Marsh Hen.

Drawn from Nature by J. J. Audubon F.R.S.F.L.S.

1. Male. 2. Female.

Lith.d Printed & Col.d by J. T. Bowen Phil.

1.

2.

Great Red-breasted Rail, or fresh water Marsh Hen

Drawn from Nature by J.J. Audubon F.R.S.F.L.S.

1. Male adult. 2. Young

Lith^d. Printed & Col^d. by J.T. Bowen, Phil^a.

No. 63

Pl. 311.

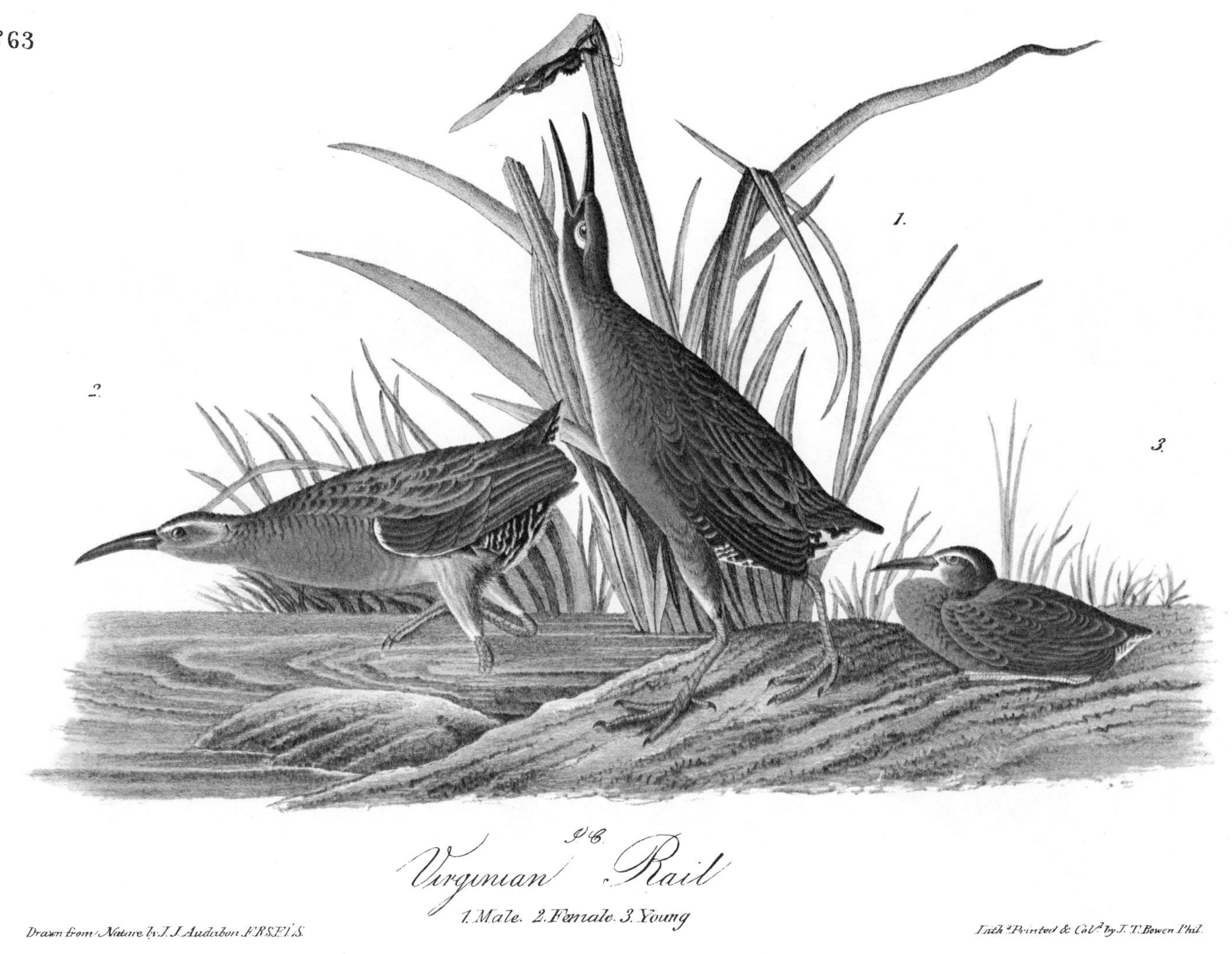

Virginian Rail

1. Male. 2. Female. 3. Young

Drawn from Nature by J. J. Audubon F.R.S.F.L.S.

Lith.d Printed & Col.d by J. T. Bowen Phil.

No. 63.
Pl. 312.
Scolopaceous Courlan
Drawn from Nature by J.J. Audubon, F.R.S. F.L.S.
Lith.d Printed & Col.d by J.T. Bowen, Phila.

No. 63. Pl. 313.

Whooping Crane.

Male, adult.

Drawn from Nature by J.J.Audubon, F.R.S.F.L.S. Lith.d Printed & Col.d by J. T. Bowen, Philad.a

N°. 63. Pl 314

Whooping Crane
Young.

Drawn from Nature by J. J. Audubon F.R.S.F.L.S. Lith.d Printed & Col.d by J. T. Bowen. Phil.

No. 64. Pl. 316.

2.

3.

1.

W. H.

American Golden Plover.

1. Summer Plumage. 2. Winter. 3. Variety in March.

Drawn from Nature by J. J. Audubon, F.R.S. F.L.S.

Lith.d Printed & Col.d by J. T. Bowen, Phil.

1. 2.

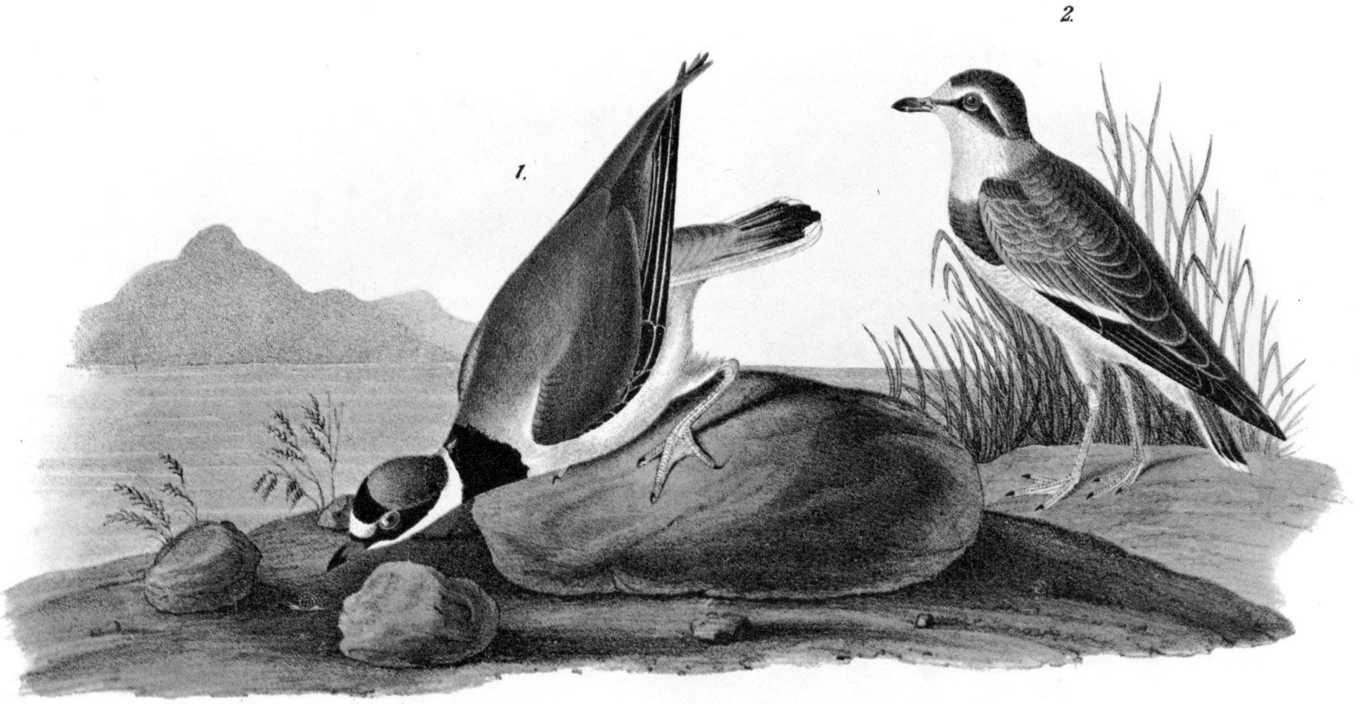

American Ring Plover.

1. Adult Male. 2. Young in August.

Drawn from Nature by J. J. Audubon F.R.S.F.L.S.

Lith.d Printed & Col.d by J. T. Bowen Phil.

Black-bellied Plover.

1. Male. 2. Young in Autumn. 3. Nestling.

Drawn from Nature by J. J. Audubon F.R.S.F.L.S.

Lith.d Printed & Col.d by J. T. Bowen Phil.

No. 64. Pl. 317.

1

2

Kildeer Plover

1. Male. 2. Female.

Drawn from Nature by J. J. Audubon. F.R.S.F.L.S.

Lith.d Printed & Col.d by J. T. Bowen. Phil.

No. 65

Pl. 321.

2.

1.

Piping W.H. Plover.

1. Male. 2. Female.

Drawn from Nature by J. J. Audubon. F.R.S. F.L.S.

Lithd. Printed & Cold. by J. T. Bowen. Phil.

N°64. Pl. 318.

Fig.

Rocky Mountain Plover.

Female.

Drawn from Nature by J.J. Audubon F.R.S.F.L.S. Lith.d Printed & Col.d by J.T. Bowen, Phil.

No. 64. Pl. 319.

Wilson's Plover.

1. Male. 2. Female.

Drawn from Nature by J. J. Audubon, F.R.S.F.L.S.

Lith.d Printed & Col.d by J. T. Bowen, Phil.

No. 65. Pl. 322.

Townsend's (W. 70) Surf-Bird.

Females.

Drawn from Nature by J. J. Audubon F.R.S.F.L.S.

Lith.d Printed & Col.d by J. T. Bowen Phil.

No. 65.

Pl 323.

1.

2.

Turnstone. 1. Summer Plumage. 2. Winter.

Drawn from Nature by J. J. Audubon, F.R.S. F.L.S.

Lith.d Printed & Col.d by J. T. Bowen, Phil.

No. 65. Pl. 324

R. T.

American Oyster-Catcher

Male.

Drawn from Nature by J. J. Audubon, F.R.S.F.L.S.

Lith.d Printed & Col.d by J. T. Bowen, Phil.

Bachman's Oyster-catcher. J.C.

Male.

Drawn from Nature by J. J. Audubon, F.R.S.F.L.S.

Lith.d Printed & Col.d by J. T. Bowen, Phil.

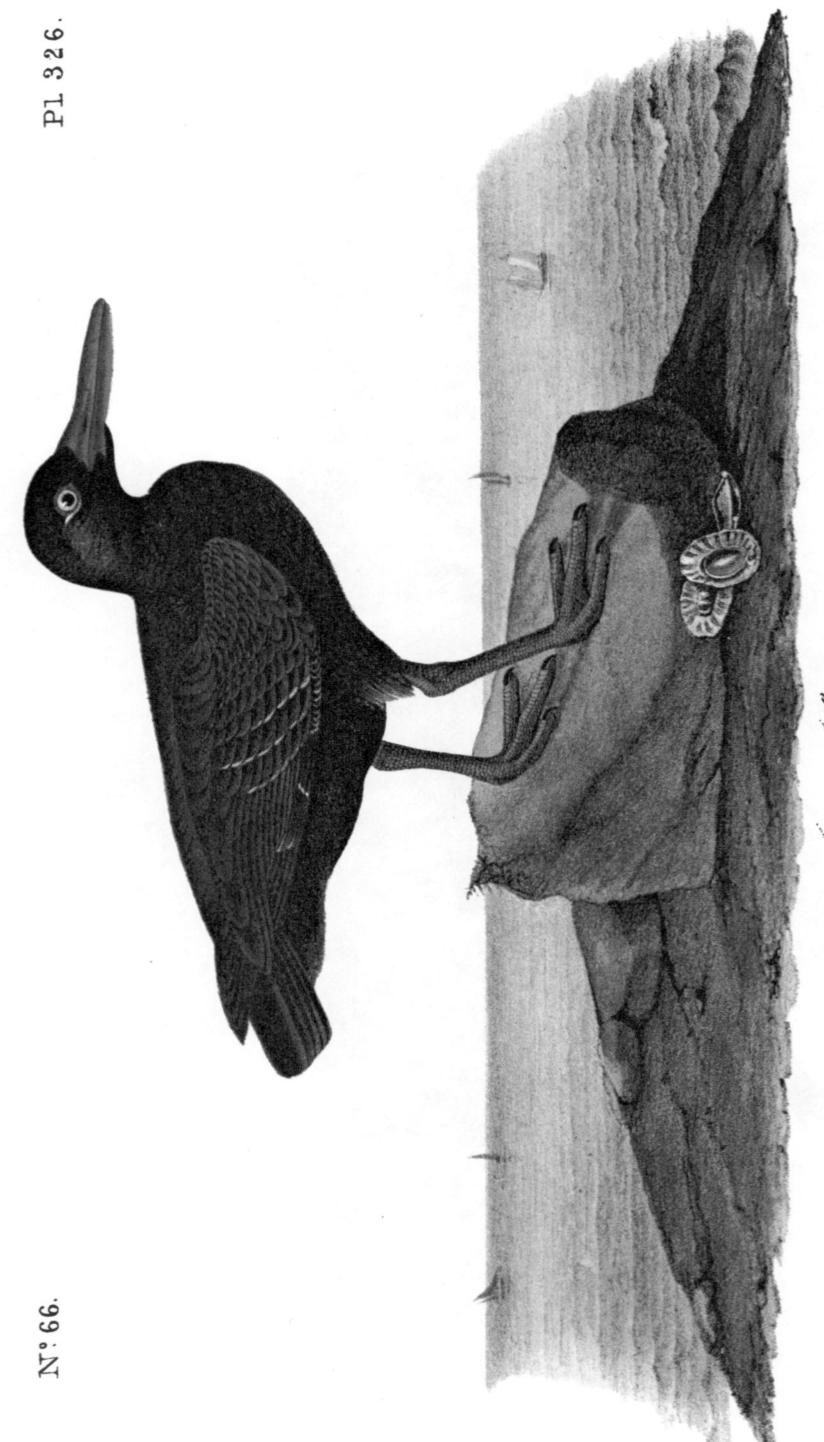
Pl 326.
Nº 66.
Townsend's Oyster-catcher?
Female
Drawn from Nature by J. J. Audubon F.R.S.F.L.S.
Lith. Printed & Col. by J. T. Bowen Phil.

2.

1.

W. H.

Bartramian Sandpiper

1. Male. 2. Female.

Drawn from Nature by J. J. Audubon, F.R.S.F.L.S.

Lithd. Printed & Cold. by J. T. Bowen, Phil.

No. 67. Pl. 331.

Buff breasted Sand-piper. R.T.

1. Male. 2. Female.

Drawn from Nature by J. J. Audubon F.R.S.F.L.S.

Lith.d Printed & Col.d by J. T. Bowen, Philad.

No. 67. Pl. 333.

Curlew Sandpiper?

1 Adult Male. 2. Young.

Drawn from Nature by J. J. Audubon. F.R.S.F.L.S.

Lith. Printed & Col. by J. T. Bowen. Phil.

1.

2.

Little Sandpiper.

1. Male. Summer plumage. 2. Female.

Drawn from Nature by J. J. Audubon F.R.S.F.L.S.

Lith.d Printed & Col.d by J. T. Bowen Phil.

N° 67.

Pl. 334.

1. 2.

Long-legged Sandpiper.

Drawn from Nature by J. J. Audubon F.R.S.F.L.S.

Lith.d Printed & Col.d by J. T. Bowen Phil.

Nº. 66.

Pl. 329.

Pectoral Sandpiper

1. Male 2. Female

Drawn from Nature by J. J. Audubon F.R.S. F.L.S.

Lith.d Printed & Col.d by J. T. Bowen, Phila.

N.º 66.
Pl. 330.
1.
2.
Purple Sandpiper.
1. Summer. 2. Winter.
Drawn from Nature by J. J. Audubon, F.R.S.F.L.S.
Lith.d Printed & Col.d by J. T. Bowen, Phil.

No. 67. Pl. 332.

Red-backed Sandpiper

1. Summer Plumage. 2. Winter.

Drawn from Nature by J. J. Audubon, F.R.S. F.L.S.

Lith. Printed & Col. by J. T. Bowen, Phil.

N° 66. Pl. 328.

W. H.

Red-breasted Sandpiper

1. Summer Plumage. 2 Winter.

Drawn from Nature by J. J. Audubon, F.R.S.F.L.S.

Lith.d Printed & Col.d by J. T. Bowen, Phil.

No. 68.

Pl. 338.

1. 2.

C. 4.
Sanderling Sandpiper.

1. Winter plumage. 2. Summer.

Drawn from Nature by J. J. Audubon, F.R.S. F.L.S.

Lith. Printed & Col.d by J. T. Bowen, Phil.

No. 67. Pl. 335.

1.

2.

Schinz's Sandpiper

1 Male. 2 Female.

Drawn from Nature by J. J. Audubon, F.R.S. F.L.S.

Lith.d Printed & Col.d by J. T. Bowen, Phila.

No. 68. Pl. 336.

Semipalmated Sandpiper.

1. Summer Plumage. 2. Winter.

Drawn from Nature by J. J. Audubon F.R.S. F.L.S.

Lith.d Printed & Col.d by J. T. Bowen, Phila.

No. 68. Pl. 339.

J. C.

Red Phalarope

1. Adult Male. 2. Winter plumage

Drawn from Nature by J. J. Audubon, F.R.S. F.L.S.

Lith.d Printed & Col.d by J. T. Bowen, Philad.

1.

2.

3.

J. C.

Hyperborean Phalarope.

1. Male. 2. Female. 3. Young in autumn.

Drawn from Nature by J. J. Audubon. F.R.S. F.L.S.

Lith.d Printed & Col.d by J. T. Bowen. Phil.

No. 69.
Pl. 341.
1.
2.
W. H.
Wilsons Phalarope.
1, Male, 2, Female.
Drawn from Nature by J. J. Audubon F.R.S. F.L.S.
Lith.d Printed & Col.d by J. T. Bowen, Phila.

No. 70. Pl. 346.

Greenshank
Male.
VIEW OF ST AUGUSTINE & SPANISH FORT FLORIDA.

Drawn from Nature by J. J. Audubon, F.R.S. F.L.S. *Lith.d Printed & Col.d by J. T. Bowen, Phila.*

No. 70.

Pl. 347.

1.

2.

W.H.

Semipalmated Snipe Willet or Stone Curlew.

1. Male Spring Plumage 2. Female in Winter

Drawn from Nature by J. J. Audubon F.R.S.F.L.S

Lith.d Printed & Col.d by J. T. Bowen Phila.

No 69. Pl. 343.

Drawn from Nature by J.J. Audubon F.R.S.F.L.S.

Solitary Sandpiper.

1, Male. 2, Female.

Lith.d Printed & Col.d by J.T. Bowen, Phila.

No. 69. Pl. 342.

2. 1.

W.H.

Spotted Sandpiper

1. Male 2. Female.

Drawn from Nature by J. J. Audubon, F.R.S. F.L.S.

Lith.d Printed & Col.d by J. T. Bowen, Phila.

No. 69.
Pl. 345.
1
2
Tell-tale Godwit or Snipe
1. Male. 2. Female.
VIEW OF EAST FLORIDA
Drawn from Nature by J.J. Audubon, F.R.S. F.L.S.
Lith.d Printed & Col.d by J.T. Bowen, Phila.

No. 69.
Pl. 344.
C.P.
Yellow Shanks Snipe.
Male, Summer Plumage.
VIEW IN SOUTH CAROLINA.
Drawn from Nature by J.J.Audubon F.R.S.F.L.S.
Lith.d Printed & Col.d by J.T.Bowen, Phila.

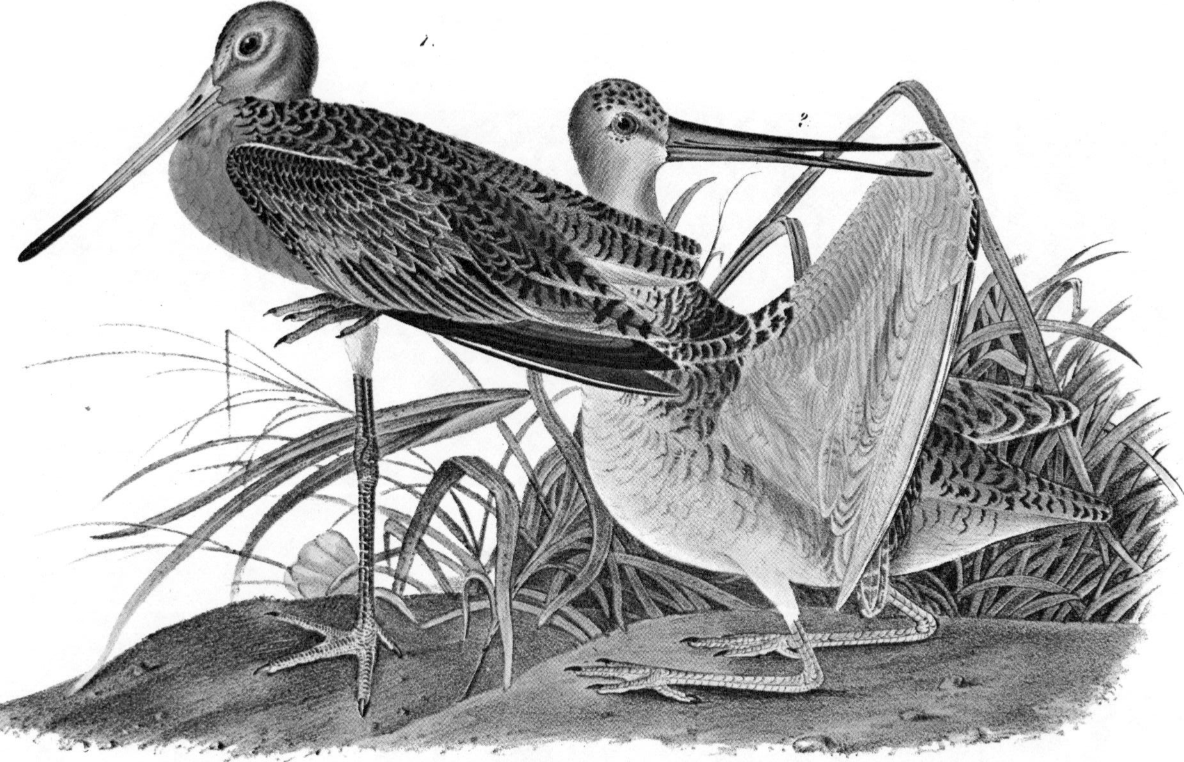

W. H.

Great Marbled Godwit.

1. Male, 2. Female.

Drawn from Nature by J. J. Audubon, F.R.S.F.L.S.

Lith.d Printed & Col.d by J. T. Bowen, Phila.

No. 70.

Pl. 349.

Hudsonian Godwit.

1. Male, 2. Female Summer Plumage

Drawn from Nature by J. J. Audubon, F.R.S. F.L.S.

Lith.d Printed & Col.d by J. T. Bowen, Phila.

No. 71.

Pl. 351.

Red-breasted Snipe.

1. Spring Plumage. 2. Winter

Drawn from Nature by J.J. Audubon, F.R.S.F.L.S.

Lith. Printed & Col. by J.T. Bowen, Phila.

No. 70. Pl. 350.

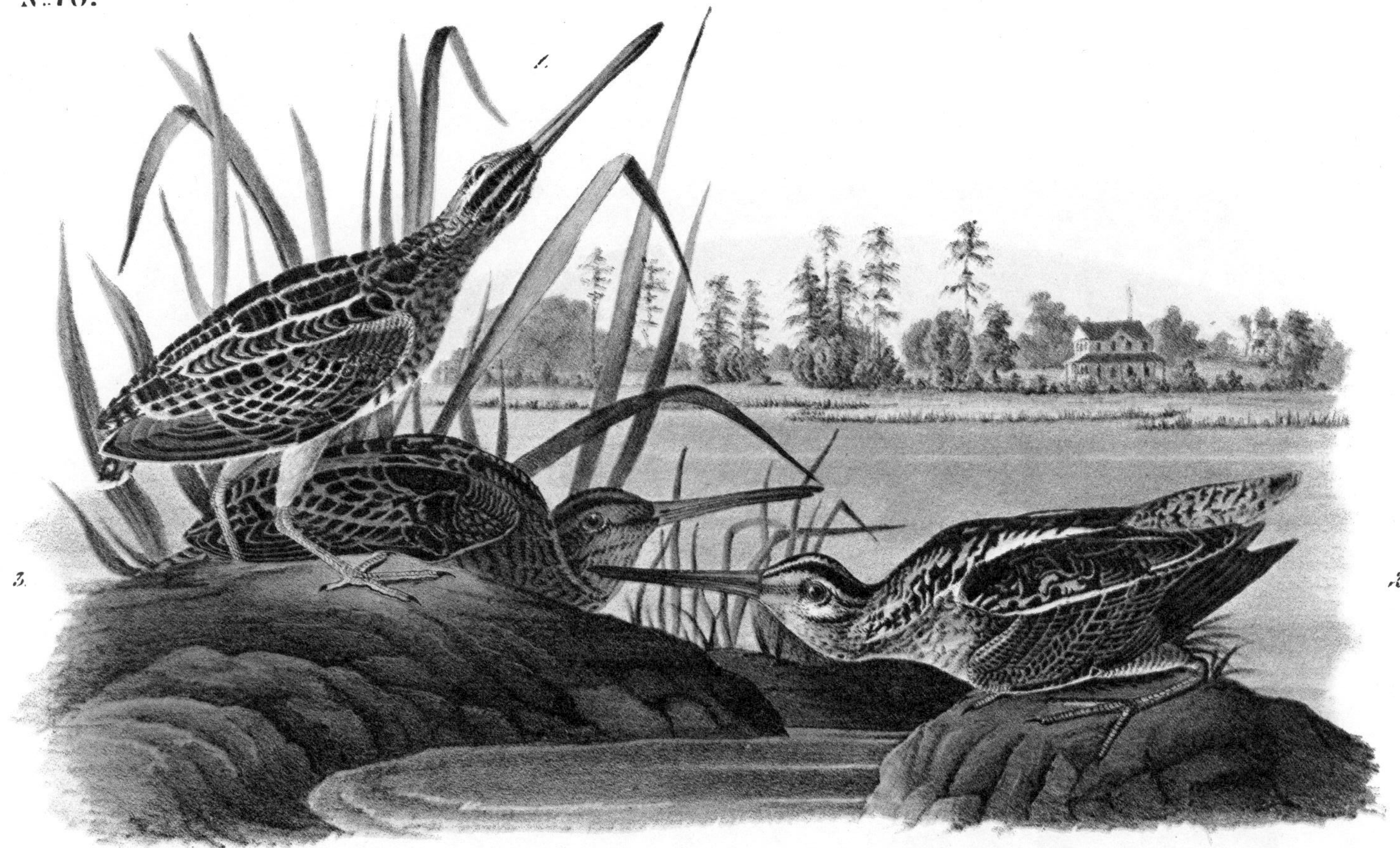

Wilson's Snipe_Common Snipe.

1. Male, 2. & 3. Females.

PLANTATION NEAR CHARLESTON, S.C.

Drawn from Nature by J.J. Audubon, F.R.S.F.L.S.

Lith.d Printed & Col.d by J.T. Bowen, Phila.

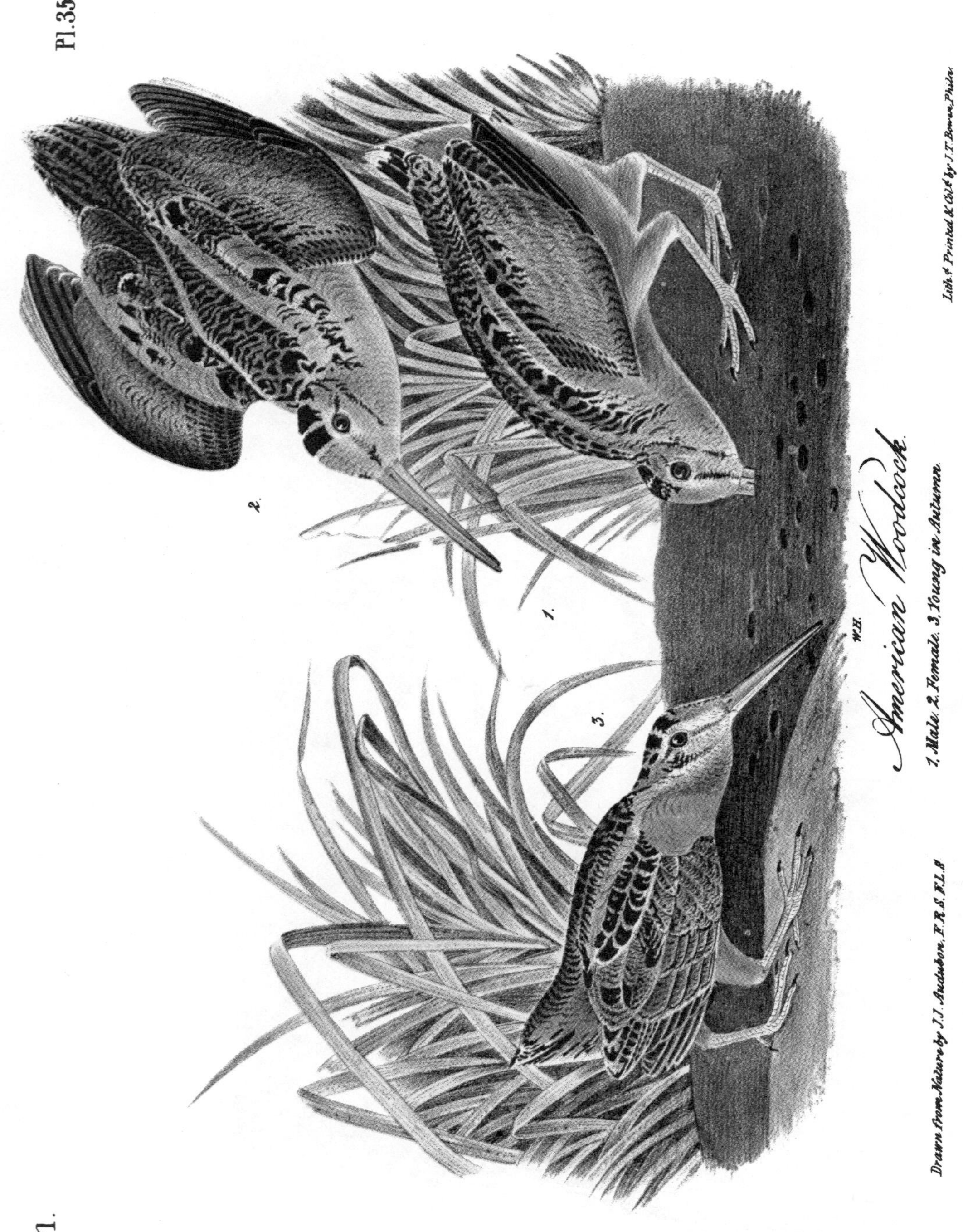

No. 71.
Pl. 352.
2.
1.
3.
W.B.
American Woodcock.
1. Male. 2. Female. 3. Young in Autumn.
Drawn from Nature by J.J. Audubon, F.R.S.F.L.S.
Lith.& Printed & Col.d by J.T. Bowen, Philad.a

C.P.

American Avocet.

Young in first Winter Plumage. Adult in the Distance.

Drawn from Nature by J. J. Audubon F.R.S. F.L.S.

Lith.d Printed & Col.d by J. T. Bowen, Phila.

No. 71.

Pl. 354.

C.P.

Black Necked Stilt

Male.

Drawn from Nature by J. J. Audubon, F.R.S. F.L.S.

Lithd. Printed & Cold. by J. T. Bowen, Phila.

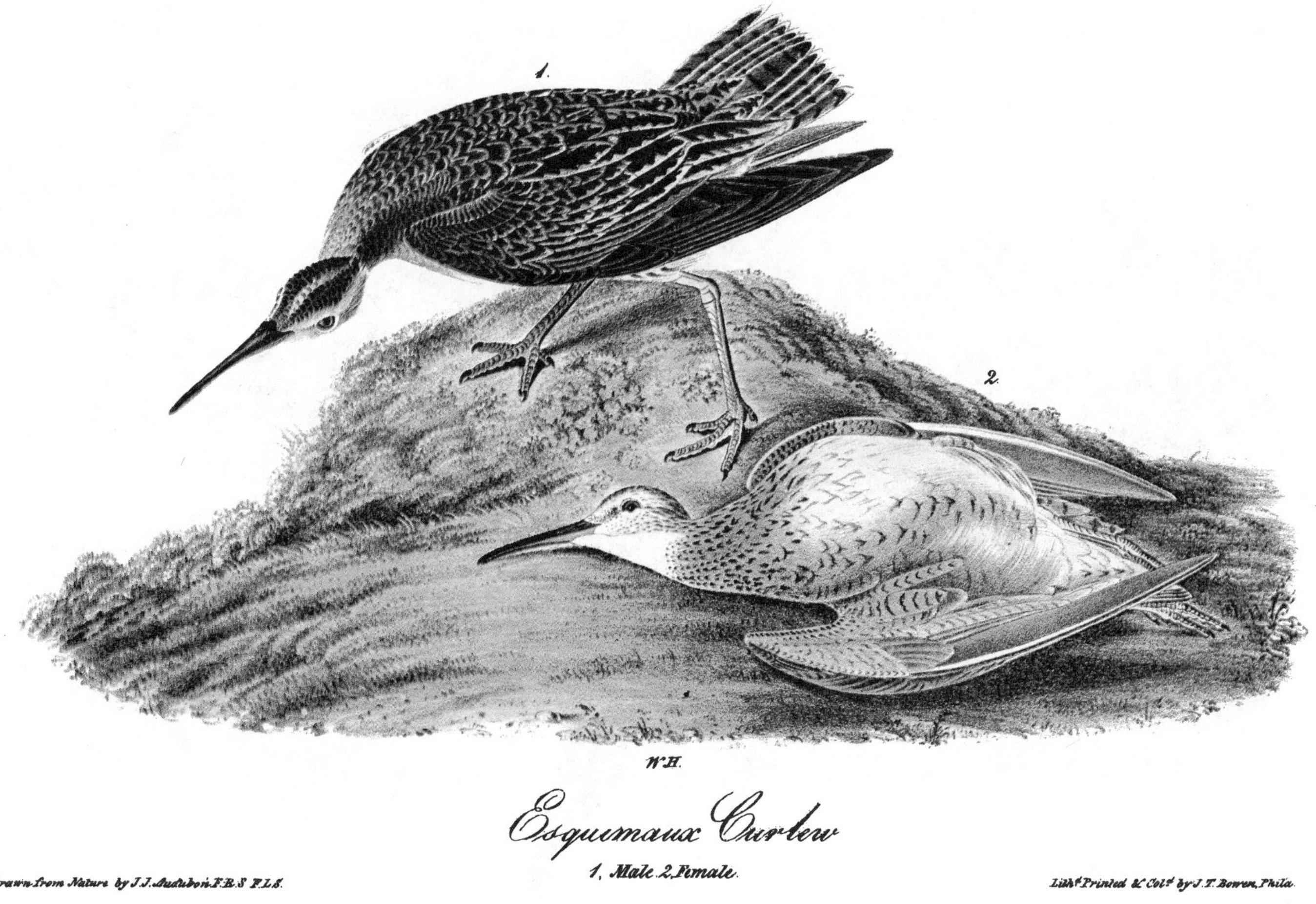

Esquimaux Curlew

1, Male. 2, Female.

Drawn from Nature by J. J. Audubon F.R.S. F.L.S.

Lithd Printed & Cold by J. T. Bowen, Phila.

No. 72.

Pl. 356.

C P

Hudsonian Curlew.

Male

Drawn from Nature by J. J. Audubon F.R.S. F.L.S.

Lith.d Printed & Col.d by J. T. Bowen, Phila.

No. 71. Pl. 355.

Long-billed Curlew.

1. Male. 2. Female.

City of Charleston.

Drawn from Nature by J.J. Audubon, F.R.S.F.L.S.

Lith.d Printed & Col.d by J. T. Bowen, Philad.a

No. 72.
Pl. 358.
Glossy Ibis
Adult Male
Drawn from Nature by J.J. Audubon F.R.S.F.L.S.
Lithd. Printed & Cold. by J.T. Bowen, Phila.

N°72.
Pl. 359.
1
2
W.H.
Scarlet Ibis.
1. Adult male 2. Young second Autumn.
Drawn from Nature by J.J. Audubon F.R.S.F.L.S.
Lith.d Printed & Col.d by J.T. Bowen, Phila.

No. 72. No. 360.

1. 2.

W.H.

White Ibis.

1, Adult, 2, Young in Autumn.

Drawn from Nature by J. J. Audubon, F.R.S. F.L.S.

Lith.d Printed & Col.d by J. T. Bowen, Phila.

No. 73. Pl. 361.

W.H.

Wood Ibis.

Male

Drawn from Nature by J.J. Audubon F.R.S F.L.S. Lith.d Printed & Col.d by J.T. Bowen, Philad.a

No. 73. Pl. 362.

W.H

Roseate Spoonbill

Male

Drawn from Nature by J. J. Audubon, F.R.S. F.L.S.

Lith.d Printed & Col.d by J. T. Bowen, Philad.a

No. 73. Pl. 365.

1.

2.

W.H.

American Bittern

1. Male. 2. Female

Drawn from Nature by J. J. Audubon, F.R.S. F.L.S.

Lith.d Printed & Col.d by J. T. Bowen, Phila.

No. 73.
Pl. 363.
Black-Crowned Night-Heron, or Qua Bird.
1. Adult. 2. Young.
Drawn from Nature by J. J. Audubon, F.R.S. F.L.S.
Lith.d Printed & Col.d by J. T. Bowen, Phila.

No. 75.

Pl. 372.

Blue Heron.

1. Male adult Spring Plumage. 2. Young second Year.

Drawn from Nature by J. J. Audubon, F.R.S. F.L.S.

Lith.d Printed & Col.d by J. T. Bowen, Philad.

No. 74

Pl. 370.

Great American White Egret.

1. Male, Spring Plumage. 2. Horned Agama Tapayaxin of Hernandes.

Drawn from Nature by J.J. Audubon, F.R.S.F.L.S.

Lith Printed & Col'd by J.T. Bowen, Phila.

Great blue Heron.

Male.

Drawn from Nature by J.J. Audubon, F.R.S.F.L.S. Lith.d Printed & Col.d by J. T. Bowen, Philad.a

No. 74. Pl. 368.

Great White Heron

Male adult, Spring Plumage.

Drawn from Nature by J. J. Audubon, F.R.S. F.L.S.

Lith. Printed & Col.d by J. T. Bowen, Philada.

No. 74.

Pl. 367

Green Heron

1. Adult Male. 2. Young in Septr

Drawn from Nature by J. J. Audubon, F.R.S. F.L.S.

Lith. Printed & Col.d by J. T. Bowen, Philad.a

1.

2.

3.

W.H.

Least Bittern

1, Male. 2, Female. 3, Young

Drawn from Nature by J. J. Audubon, F.R.S.F.L.S.

Lith.d Printed & Col.d by J. T. Bowen, Phila.

No. 75. Pl. 373.

Louisiana Heron.

Drawn from Nature by J.J. Audubon, F.R.S.F.L.S.

Male Adult.

Lith.d Printed & Col.d by J. T. Bowen, Philad.a

No. 75. Pl. 371.

Reddish Egret

1. Adult, full Spring Plumage. 2. Young in full Spring Plumage two Years old.

Drawn from Nature by J. J. Audubon, F.R.S.F.L.S. Lith. Printed & Col.d by J. T. Bowen, Phila.

No75. | Pl. 374.

C.P

Snowy Heron

Male.

Drawn from Nature by J. J. Audubon. F.R.S. F.L.S.

Lith. Printed & Col.d by J. T. Bowen, Phila.

No. 73. Pl. 364.

C.P.

Yellow Crowned Night Heron

Drawn from Nature by J. J. Audubon, F.R.S. F.L.S. 1. Adult Male, Spring Plumage 2. Young in October. Lithd., Printed & Cold. by J. T. Bowen, Phila.

American Flamingo.

Adult Male.

Drawn from Nature by J. J. Audubon F.R.S. F.L.S.

Lith. Printed & Colᵈ by J. T. Bowen Phila.

1.

2.

Bernacle Goose

1. Male. 2. Female

Drawn from Nature by J. J. Audubon F.R.S.F.L.S.

Lith. Printed & Col.d by J. T. Bowen, Phila.

No. 76.
Pl. 379.
2
W.H.
Brant Goose
1. Male 2. Female
Drawn from Nature by J.J. Audubon, F.R.S.F.L.S.
Lith.d Printed & Col.d by J.T. Bowen, Philad.a

N°. 76.　　　　　Pl. 376.

Canada Goose.

1. Male 2. Female

Drawn from Nature by J. J. Audubon F.R.S.F.L.S.

No. 76.
Pl. 380.
1.
2.
W.H.
White-fronted Goose.
1. Male. 2. Female.
Drawn from Nature by J.J. Audubon, F.R.S. F.L.S.
Lith. Printed & Col.d by J.T. Bowen, Philad.a

No. 76. Pl. 377.

C.P.

Hutchins's Goose.

Adult Male

Drawn from Nature by J.J. Audubon, F.R.S.F.L.S. Lith.d Printed & Col.d by J.T. Bowen, Philad.a

No. 77. Pl. 381.

W.H.

Snow Goose

1. Adult male. 2. Young Female.

Drawn from Nature by J. J. Audubon, F.R.S. F.L.S.

Lith. Printed & Col.d by J. T. Bowen, Phila.

No. 77. Pl. 384.

American Swan.

Male

Drawn from Nature by J. J. Audubon, F.R.S. F.L.S.

Lith. Printed & Col.d by J. T. Bowen, Phila.

No. 77. Pl. 382.

Trumpeter Swan.

Adult.

Drawn from Nature by J. J. Audubon, F.R.S. F.L.S.

Lith. Printed & Col^d by J. T. Bowen, Phila.

No. 77. Pl. 383.

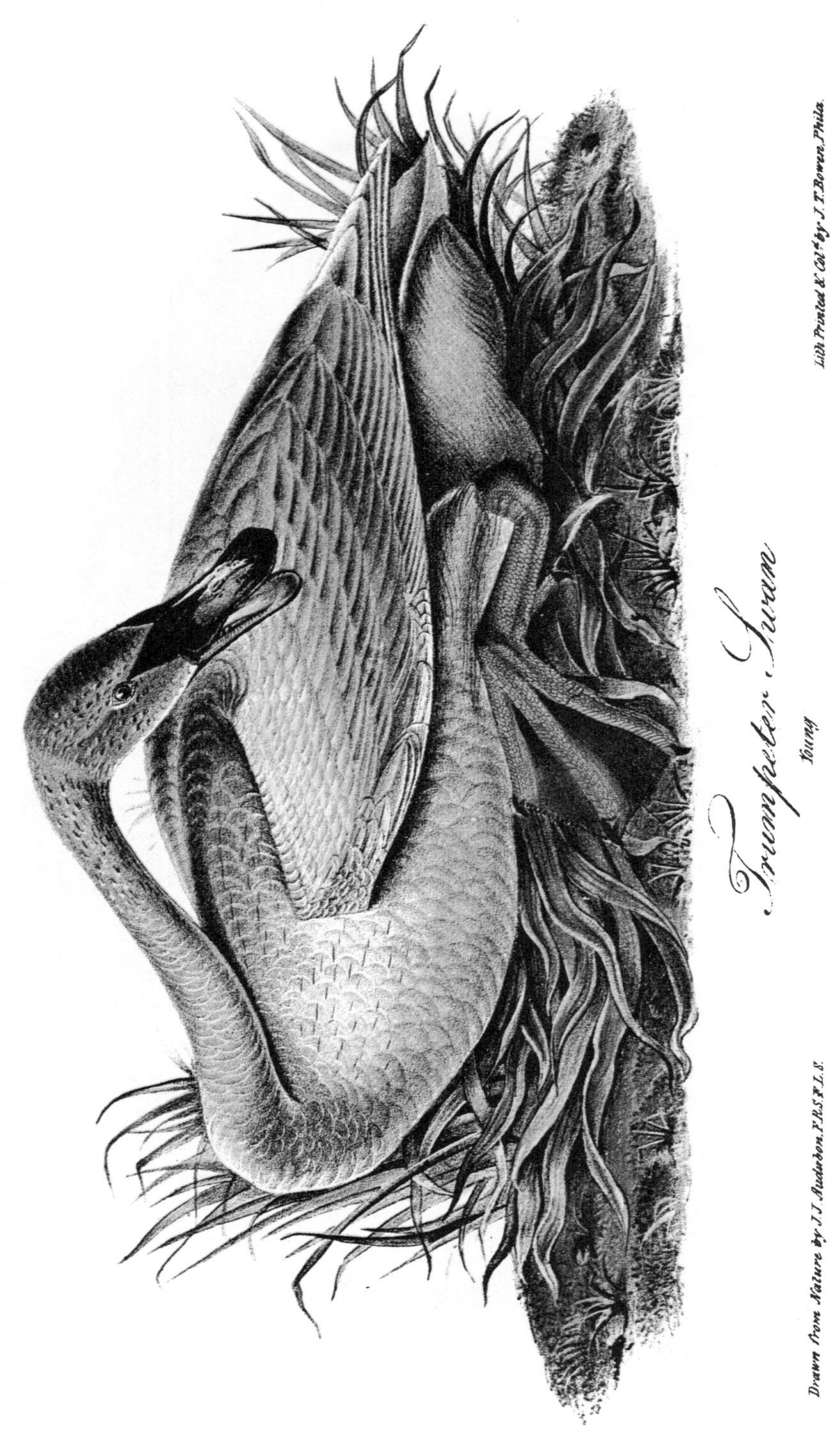

Trumpeter Swan

Young

Drawn from Nature by J.J. Audubon, F.R.S.F.L.S. Lith. Printed & Col.d by J.T. Bowen, Phila.

No. 78.

Pl. 389.

American Widgeon

1. Male 2. Female.

Drawn from Nature by J.J. Audubon F.R.S.F.L.S.

Lith. Printed & Col.d by J.T. Bowen, Phila.

No. 79. Pl. 392.

American Green-winged Teal.

Drawn from Nature by J. J. Audubon, F.R.S. F.L.S.

1. Male, 2. Female.

Lith. Printed & Col.d by J. T. Bowen, Phila.

No. 79. Pl. 393.

Blue-winged Teale

Drawn from Nature by J.J.Audubon, F.R.S.F.L.S. 1. Male. 2. Female. Lith.d Printed & Col.d by J. T. Bowen, Philad.a

No. 78. Pl. 387.

R.T.

Brewers Duck.

Male

Drawn from Nature by J. J. Audubon, F.R.S. F.L.S.

Lith. Printed & Col.d by J. T. Bowen, Phila.

No. 78. Pl. 386.

1

2

Duskey Duck.

1. Male 2. Female

Drawn from Nature by J. J. Audubon F.R.S. F.L.S.

Lith. Printed & Col.d by J. T. Bowen, Phila.

No. 78.

Pl. 388.

Gadwall Duck.

1. Male. 2. Female.

Drawn from Nature by J. J. Audubon, F.R.S. F.L.S.

Lith. Printed & Col.d by J. T. Bowen, Phila.

No. 77. Pl. 385.

C.P.

Mallard

1, 2, Males. 3, 4, Females

Drawn from Nature by J. J. Audubon, F.R.S.F.L.S.

Lith.d Printed & Col.d by J. T. Bowen, Philad.a

No. 78.

Pl. 390

2.

1.

C.P.

Pintail Duck.

Drawn from Nature by J.J. Audubon, F.R.S.F.L.S.

1. Male. 2. Female.

Lith.d Printed & Col.d by J. T. Bowen, Philad.a

No. 79

Pl. 394

Shoveller Duck

Drawn from Nature by J.J.Audubon, F.R.S.F.L.S.

1 Male 2 Female.

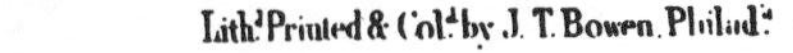
Lith.d Printed & Col.d by J. T. Bowen, Philad.a

Wood Duck — Summer Duck.

1. Male, 2. Female.

Drawn from Nature by J. J. Audubon, F.R.S. F.L.S.

Lith. Printed & Col.d by J. T. Bowen, Phila.

1.

2.

W.H.

American Scoter Duck.

1. Male. 2. Female.

Drawn from Nature by J. J. Audubon, F.R.S. F.L.S.

Lith. Printed & Col.d by J. T. Bowen, Philad.a

No. 81. Pl. 402.

Black or Surf Duck.

1. Male 2. Female.

Drawn from Nature by J. J. Audubon F.R.S. F.L.S.

Lith. Printed & Col^d by J. T. Bowen Philad^a

No. 82. Pl. 108

1.

2.

W.H.

Buffel-headed Duck

1. Male. 2. Female.

Drawn from Nature by J. J. Audubon, F.R.S. F.L.S.

Lith. Printed & Col.d by J. T. Bowen, Phila.

C.P.

Canvass Back Duck

1 Male 2 Female

VIEW OF BALTIMORE, MARYLAND

Drawn from Nature by J.J. Audubon, F.R.S.F.L.S.

Lith.d Printed & Col.d by J. T. Bowen, Philad.a

No. 100. Pl. 498.

1.

2.

W.E.H.

Common Scaup Duck

1, Male. 2, Female.

Drawn from Nature by J. J. Audubon, F.R.S. F.L.S.

Lith. Printed & Col.d by J. T. Bowen, Philad.a

No. 81. Pl. 405.

Eider Duck.

1, Male. 2, Female.

Drawn from Nature by J. J. Audubon F.R.S. F.L.S.

Lith. Printed & Col.d by J. T. Bowen, Phila.

No. 82. Pl. 406.

Golden Eye Duck

1. Male. 2. Female.

Drawn from Nature by J. J. Audubon, F.R.S.F.L.S.

Lith. Printed & Col.d by J. T. Bowen, Philad.a

No. 82. Pl. 409.

1. 2. 3.

W.H.

Harlequin Duck

1, old Male, 2, Female, 3, Young Male

Drawn from Nature by J. J. Audubon, F.R.S. F.L.S.

Lith. Printed & Col.d by J. T. Bowen, Philad.a

No. 81. Pl. 404.

Drawn from Nature by J. J. Audubon, F.R.S. F.L.S

King Duck.
1. Male. 2. Female.

Lith. Printed & Col'd by J. T. Bowen, Phila.

Long-tailed Duck.

1. Male, Summer Plumage, 2. Male in Winter. 3. Female and Young.

Drawn from Nature by J. J. Audubon, F.R.S.F.L.S

Lith. Printed & Col.d by J. T. Bowen, Philad.a

No. 80.

Pl. 400.

1.

2.

W.H.

Pied Duck.

1. Male 2. Female

Drawn from Nature by J. J. Audubon, F.R.S. F.L.S.

Lith. Printed & Col[d]. by J. T. Bowen, Phila.

No. 80. Pl. 396

1. 2.

W. H.

Red-headed Duck.

1. Male. 2. Female.

Drawn from Nature by J. J. Audubon, F.R.S.F.L.S.

Lith.d Printed & Col.d by J. T. Bowen, Philad.a

No. 80. Pl. 398.

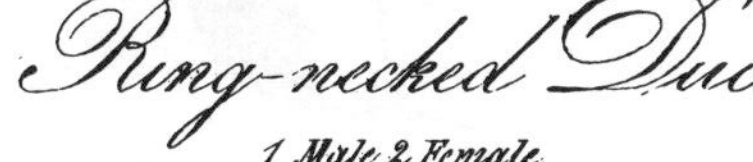

R.T.

Ring-necked Duck

1, Male. 2, Female.

Drawn from Nature by J. J. Audubon, F.R.S. F.L.S.

Lith. Printed & Col^{d} by J. T. Bowen, Philad^{a}

No. 80. Pl. 399.

1. 3. 3 2.

W.H.

Ruddy Duck

1, Male. 2, Female. 3, Young.

Drawn from Nature by J. J. Audubon, F.R.S. F.L.S.

Lith. Printed & Col.d by J. T. Bowen, Philad.a

No. 80. Pl. 397.

Scaup Duck.

1. Male. 2. Female.

Drawn from Nature by J. J. Audubon, F.R.S. F.L.S.

Lith. Printed & Col.d by J. T. Bowen, Philad.a

Velvet Duck.

1. Male. 2. Female.

Drawn from Nature by J.J. Audubon, F.R.S. F.L.S.

Lith. Printed & Col.d by J.T. Bowen, Phila.

No. 82.

Pl. 407.

C.P.

Western Duck.

Males

Drawn from Nature by J. J. Audubon, F.R.S.F.L.S.

Lith. Printed & Col.d by J. T. Bowen, Philad.a

No. 83. Pl. 411.

Buff-breasted Merganser - Goosander

1. Male. 2. Female

Drawn from Nature by J. J. Audubon, F.R.S.F.L.S. Lith. Printed & Col.d by J. T. Bowen, Philad.a

No. 83.

Pl. 413.

Hooded Merganser.

1, Male. 2, Female.

Drawn from Nature by J.J. Audubon, F.R.S. F.L.S.

Lith. Printed & Col^{d} by J.T. Bowen Philad^{a}

No. 83. Pl. 412.

2.

1.

W.H.

Red-breasted Merganser.

1. Male. 2. Female.

Drawn from Nature by J. J. Audubon, F.R.S. F.L.S.

Lith. Printed & Col.d by J. T. Bowen, Philad.a

White Merganser - Smew White Nun

1. Male. 2. Female.

Drawn from Nature by J.J. Audubon F.R.S. F.L.S. Lith. Printed & Col.d by J.T. Bowen, Philad.a

N° 83. Pl. 415.

3. 3 C.P

Common Cormorant

1. Male. 2. Female. 3. Young.

Drawn from Nature by J. J. Audubon, F.R.S. F.L.S.

Lith. Printed & Col.d by J. T. Bowen, Philada.

Double-crested Cormorant

Male

Drawn from Nature by J. J. Audubon, F.R.S. F.L.S.

Lith. Printed & Col.d by J. T. Bowen, Philad.a

No. 84. Pl. 417.

Florida Cormorant

Male

Drawn from Nature by J. J. Audubon, F.R.S. F.L.S.

Lith. Printed & Col.d by J. T. Bowen, Phila.

W. H.

Townsend's Cormorant

Male

Drawn from Nature by J. J. Audubon, F.R.S. F.L.S.

Lith. Printed & Col[d] by J. T. Bowen, Phila.

Violet green Cormorant

Drawn from Nature by J. J. Audubon F.R.S.F.L.S. Female in Winter Lith. Printed & Col.d by J. T. Bowen, Philad.a

No. 84. Pl. 420.

American Anhinga Snake Bird

1. Male 2. Female

Drawn from Nature by J. J. Audubon F.R.S. F.L.S. Lith Printed & Col.d by J. T. Bowen Phila

Frigate Pelican. Man of War Bird.

Male.

Drawn from Nature by J. J. Audubon F.R.S. F.L.S. Lith Printed & Col^{d} by J. T. Bowen Phila.

American White Pelican

Male.

Drawn from Nature by J.J. Audubon, F.R.S.F.L.S.

Lith.d Printed & Col.d by J. T. Bowen, Philad.a

Brown Pelican.

Drawn from Nature by J J Audubon F R S F L S

Adult Male

Lith Printed & Col.d by J T Bowen, Philadelphia

No. 85. Pl. 424.

Brown Pelican

Young first Winter.

Drawn from Nature by J. J. Audubon, F.R.S. F.L.S.

Lith. Printed & Col.d by J. T. Bowen, Philad.a

C.P.

Booby Gannet.

Male.

Drawn from Nature by J J Audubon, F.R.S. F.L.S.

Lith. Printed & Col.d by J. T. Bowen, Philada.

No. 85. Pl. 425.

Common Gannet

1. Adult male. 2. Young.

Drawn from Nature by J. J. Audubon F.R.S.F.L.S. Lith. Printed & Col.d by J. T. Bowen, Philad.a

No. 86. Pl. 427.

1.

2

Tropic Bird

1. Male 2. Female

Drawn from Nature by J. J. Audubon, F.R.S. F.L.S.

Lith. Printed & Col.d by J. T. Bowen, Phila.

No. 86. | Pl. 428.

Black Skimmer or Shearwater.

Male.

Drawn from Nature by J. J. Audubon, F.R.S. F.L.S.

Lith. Printed & Col.d by J. T. Bowen, Philad.a

Arctic Tern.

Male

Drawn from Nature by J. J. Audubon, F.R.S. F.L.S.

Lith. Printed & Col.d by J. T. Bowen, Phila.

No. 88. Pl. 438.

Black Tern.

Drawn from Nature by J. J. Audubon, F.R.S.F.L.S. 1. Adult. 2. Young Lith. Printed & Col.d by J. T. Bowen, Philad.a

No. 86. Pl. 429.

Cayenne Tern

Male.

Drawn from Nature by J. J. Audubon, F.R.S. F.L.S.

Lith. Printed & Col.d by J. T. Bowen, Philad.a

Common Tern

Male. Spring Plumage

Drawn from Nature by J. J. Audubon. F.R.S. F.L.S.

Lith. Printed & Col.d by J. T. Bowen, Phila.

Gull billed Tern Marsh Tern.

Male.

Drawn from Nature by J. J. Audubon, F.R.S. F.L.S. Lith. Printed & Col.d by J. T. Bowen, Philad.a

C.P.

Havell's Tern

Adult.

Drawn from Nature by J. J. Audubon F.R.S.F.L.S.

Lith. Printed & Col.d by J. T. Bowen, Philada.

Least Tern.

1. Adult in Spring 2. Young.

Drawn from Nature by J. J. Audubon, F.R.S.F.L.S. Lith.d Printed & Col.d by J. T. Bowen, Philad.a

No. 88. Pl. 440.

Noddy Tern

Male.

Drawn from Nature by J. J. Audubon, F.R.S. F.L.S.

Lith. Printed & Col.d by J. T. Bowen, Philad.a

No. 88. Pl. 437.

Roseate Tern.

Male.

Drawn from Nature by J. J. Audubon, F.R.S. F.L.S.

Lith. Printed & Col.d by J. T. Bowen, Philada.

No. 87.
Pl. 431.
Sandwich Tern.
Adult
Drawn from Nature by J. J. Audubon, F.R.S.F.L.S.
Lith. Printed & Col.d by J. T. Bowen, Phila.

No. 87.

Pl. 432.

Sooty Tern.

Drawn from Nature by J. J. Audubon F.R.S. F.L.S.

Lith. Printed & Col.d by J. T. Bowen, Phila.

No 87. PL. 435.

CP

Trudeau's Tern.

Adult

Drawn from Nature by J. J. Audubon F.R.S.F.L.S.

Lith. Printed & Colᵈ by J. T. Bowen, Phila.

No. 89. Pl. 443.

Black-headed Gull.

1. Adult Male Spring Plumage 2. Young first Autumn

Drawn from Nature by J. J. Audubon, F.R.S. F.L.S. Lith. Printed & Col.d by J. T. Bowen, Phila.

No. 89.
1
Pl. 442.
2
3
WII.
Bonapartes Gull.
1. Male in Spring 2. Female 3. Young first Autumn
Drawn from Nature by J. J. Audubon, F.R.S.F.L.S.
Lith. Printed & Col.d by J. T. Bowen, Philad.a

No. 90. Pl. 446.

Common American Gull_Ring-billed Gull

1. Adult 2. Young

Drawn from Nature by J. J. Audubon, F.R.S. F.L.S.

No. 89. Pl. 441.

Fork-tailed Gull

Male

Drawn from Nature by J. J. Audubon F.R.S. F.L.S.

Lith. Printed & Col.d by J. T. Bowen, Philad.a

No. 90. Pl. 449.

W.E.H.

Glaucus Gull.—Burgomaster

1. Adult male. 2. Young first Autumn.

Drawn from Nature by J. J. Audubon, F.R.S. F.L.S.

Lith. Printed & Col.d by J. T. Bowen, Phila.

W.E.H.

Great Black-backed Gull

Male

Drawn from Nature by J. J. Audubon, F.R.S.F.L.S.

Lith. Printed & Col.d by J. T. Bowen, Philada.

No. 90. Pl. 448.

Herring or Silvery Gull

1, Adult in Spring. _ 2, Young in Autumn.

Drawn from Nature by J. J. Audubon, F.R.S. F.L.S. Lith. Printed & Col^{d} by J. T. Bowen, Philadelphia.

No. 89. Pl. 445.

Ivory Gull.

1. Adult Male. 2. Young second Autumn.

Drawn from Nature by J. J. Audubon, F.R.S. F.L.S.

Lith. Printed & Col.d by J. T. Bowen, Philad.a

No. 89. Pl. 444.

2. 1.

Kittiwake Gull.

1, Adult. _ 2, Young.

Drawn from Nature by J. J. Audubon, F.R.S. F.L.S.

Lith. Printed & Col.d by J. T. Bowen, Philad.a

No. 90.
Pl. 447.
2
1
White-winged Silvery Gull
1. Male in Summer. 2. Young in Winter
Drawn from Nature by J.J. Audubon, F.R.S. F.L.S.
Lith. Printed & Col.d by J.T. Bowen, Philadelphia

No. 91. Pl. 453.

W.E.H.

Arctic Jager.

Drawn from Nature by J. J. Audubon, F.R.S. F.L.S. Lith. Printed & Col.d by J. T. Bowen, Philad.a

No. 91. Pl. 451.

W.E.H.

Pomerine Jager.

Adult Female.

Drawn from Nature by J. J. Audubon, F.R.S. F.L.S. Lith. Printed & Col.d by J. T. Bowen, Phila.

No. 91. Pl. 452.

Richardson Jager.

1. Male Adult. 2. Young in Septr.

Drawn from Nature by J.J. Audubon, F.R.S.F.L.S.

Lith. Printed & Col.d by J.T. Bowen, Philada.

No. 91. Pl. 454.

W.E.H.

Dusky Albatross.

Drawn from Nature by J. J. Audubon F.R.S. F.L.S.

Lith. Printed & Col.d by J. T. Bowen, Philad.a

No. 91. Pl. 455.

Fulmar Petrel.

Adult Male Summer Plumage.

Drawn from Nature by J. J. Audubon, F.R.S. F.L.S.

Lith. Printed & Col.d by J. T. Bowen, Philada.

No. 92.

Pl. 458.

W.E.H.

Dusky Shearwater.

Male in Spring.

Drawn from Nature by J. J. Audubon, F.R.S. F.L.S.

Lith. Printed & Col.d by J. T. Bowen, Philad.a

No. 92. Pl. 457.

Manks Shearwater

Male.

Drawn from Nature by J. J. Audubon, F.R.S. F.L.S.

Lith. Printed & Col.d by J. T. Bowen, Philada.

No. 92. Pl. 456.

Wandering Shearwater

Male

Drawn from Nature by J.J. Audubon, F.R.S.F.L.S.

Lith. Printed & Col.d by J.T. Bowen, Philad.a

No. 92. Pl. 459.

Leach's Petrel. Forked-tailed Petrel.

1. Male. 2. Female.

Drawn from Nature by J. J. Audubon, F.R.S. F.L.S.

Lith. Printed & Col.d by J. T. Bowen, Philad.a

No. 93. Pl. 461.

Least Petrel—Mother Carey's chicken.

1. Male. 2. Female.

Drawn from Nature by J. J. Audubon, F.R.S. F.L.S.

Lith. Printed & Col.d by J. T. Bowen, Philada.

N°.92.
Pl.460.
1
2
W.E.H.
Wilson's Petrel._Mother Carey's chicken.
1. Male. 2. Female
Drawn from Nature by J.J.Audubon, F.R.S.F.L.S.
Lith. Printed & Col.d by J.T. Bowen, Philada

No. 93. Pl. 464.

1

2

R.T.

Common or Arctic Puffin

1. Male. 2, Female.

Drawn from Nature by J. J. Audubon, F.R.S. F.L.S.

Lith. Printed & Col.d by J. T. Bowen, Philad.a

No. 93. Pl. 463.

Large billed Puffin.

1. Male 2. Female

Drawn from Nature by J. J. Audubon, F.R.S. F.L.S.

Lith. Printed & Col^d by J. T. Bowen, Philad^a

No. 93. Pl. 462.

Tufted Puffin.

1. Male 2. Female.

Drawn from Nature by J. J. Audubon, F.R.S. F.L.S.

Lith. Printed & Col.d by J. T. Bowen, Philada.

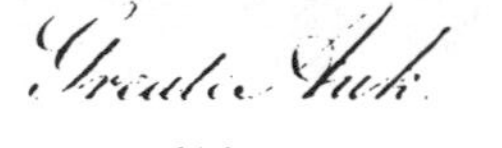

W.E.H.

Great Auk.

Adult.

Drawn from Nature by J. J. Audubon F.R.S.F.L.S.

No. 94. Pl. 466.

2

1

W.E.H.

Razor-billed Auk.

1 Male. 2 Female.

Drawn from Nature by J. J. Audubon, F.R.S.F.L.S. Lith. Printed & Col.d by J. T. Bowen, Philad.a

No. 94. Pl. 467.

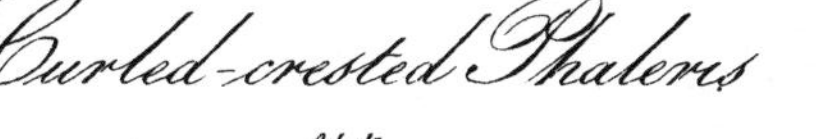

R T

Curled-crested Phaleris

Adult

Drawn from Nature by J J Audubon, F.R.S. F.L.S.

Lith. Printed & Col.d by J T Bowen Philad.a

R.T.

Knobbed-billed Phaleris.

Adult

Drawn from Nature by J. J. Audubon, F.R.S. F.L.S.

Lith. Printed & Col.d by J. T. Bowen, Philada.

No. 94. Pl. 469.

1. 2.

W.E.H.

Little Auk_Sea dove.

1. Male. 2. Female

Drawn from Nature by J. J. Audubon, F.R.S. F.L.S. Lith. Printed & Col.d by J. T. Bowen Phila.

No. 95. Pl. 474.

W.E.H.

Black Guillemot

1, Adult — Summer Plumage. 2, Adult in Winter. — 3, Young.

Drawn from Nature by J. J. Audubon, F.R.S.F.L.S.

Lith. Printed & Col.d by J. T. Bowen, Philada.

No 94
Pl. 470.
Black-throated Guillemot
1 Adult 2 Young

No. 95. Pl. 473.

Foolish Guillemot. Murre.

1. Male. 2. Female.

Drawn from Nature by J. J. Audubon, F.R.S. F.L.S.

Lith. Printed & Col.d by J. T. Bowen, Philad.a

W.R.H.

Horned-billed Guillemot

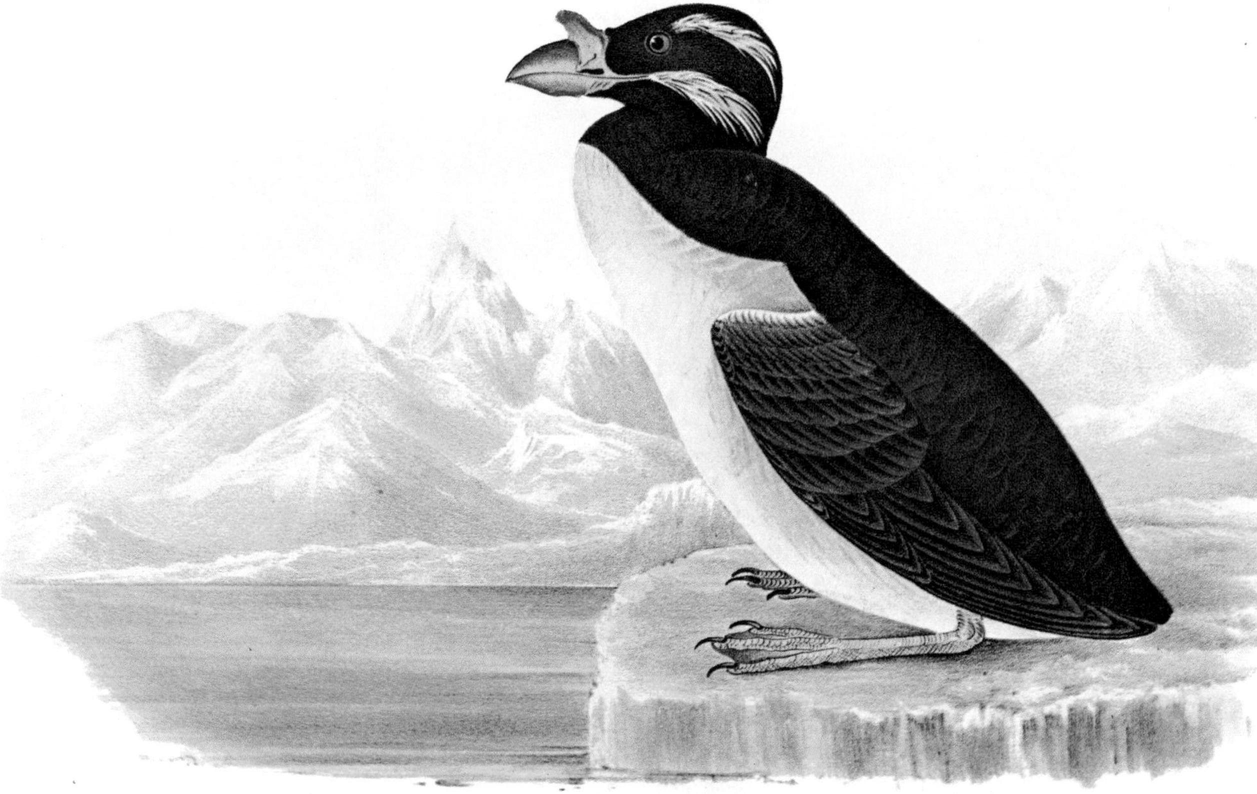

Adult

Drawn from Nature by J. J. Audubon F.R.S. F.L.S.

Lith. Printed & Col.d by J. T. Bowen, Philad.a

No. 95. Pl. 472.

W.E.H.

Large-billed Guillemot.

Male.

Drawn from Nature by J. J. Audubon, F.R.S. F.L.S.

Lith. Printed & Col.d by J. T. Bowen, Philad.a

No. 95. Pl. 475.

Slender-billed Guillemot.

1. Male. 2. Female

Drawn from Nature by J. J. Audubon, F.R.S.F.L.S.

Lith. Printed & Col.d by J. T. Bowen, Philad.a

No. 96. Pl. 477.

1. 2. 3.

W.E.H.

Black-throated Diver

1. Male. 2. Female. 3. Young in Octor.

Drawn from Nature by J. J. Audubon. F.R.S. F.L.S.

Lith. Printed & Colᵈ by J. T. Bowen, Phila.

No. 96. Pl. 476.

1

2

Great North^n Diver — Loon. W.E.H.

1 Adult. 2 Young in Winter

Drawn from Nature by J. J. Audubon F.R.S. F.L.S.

Lith. Printed & Col.^d by J. T. Bowen, Philad.^a

No. 96. Pl. 478.

Red-throated Diver.

1. Male Summer Plumage 2, do Winter 3, Female 4, Young

Drawn from Nature by J J Audubon, F.R.S.F.L.S.

Lith. Printed & Col.d by J. T. Bowen, Philad.a

No. 96. Pl. 479.

W.E.H

Crested Grebe.

1. Adult Male in Spring. 2. Young (first Winter.)

Drawn from Nature by J. J. Audubon, F.R.S. F.L.S.

Lith. Printed & Col.d by J. T. Bowen, Phila.

No. 97. Pl. 482.

Eared Grebe.

1 Male 2 Young - first Year

Drawn from Nature by J. J. Audubon, F.R.S. F.L.S.

Lith. Printed & Col^{d} by J. T. Bowen, Philad^{a}

No. 97. Pl. 481.

W.E.H.

Horned Grebe

1, Adult Male. 2, Female in Winter.

Drawn from Nature by J. J. Audubon, F.R.S. F.L.S.

Lith. Printed & Col.d by J. T. Bowen, Philad.a

No. 97. Pl. 483.

Pied-billed Dobchick

1. Male, 2. Female.

Drawn from Nature by J. J. Audubon F.R.S F.L.S

Lith. Printed & Colᵈ by J. T. Bowen, Philadᵃ

No. 96. Pl. 480.

W.E.H.

Red-necked Grebe.

Drawn from Nature by J. J. Audubon, F.R.S. F.L.S.

1. Adult Male Spring Plumage 2. Young Winter Plumage

Lith. Printed & Col^d. by J. T. Bowen, Philad^a.

BOOK OF MAMMALS

N° 16

Plate LXXVII

On Stone by W^m. E. Hitchcock

Prong-Horned Antelope.

Drawn from Nature by J.W. Audubon

Lith. Printed & Col^d. by J.T. Bowen, Phil.

No. 25. Plate CXXIII.

Drawn from Nature by J.W.Audubon

On Stone by W.E.Hitchcock

Lith.d Printed & Col.d by J.T.Bowen, Philad.a

The Sewellel.

No. 21.

Plate CIII

Drawn from Nature by J. W. Audubon.

Hoary Marmot The Whistler.

Lith. Printed & Cold. by J. T. Bowen, Phil.

N° 22

Plate CVII

Drawn on Stone by Wm. E. Hitchcock

Drawn from Nature by J.W. Audubon

Lewis' Marmot.

Lith. Printed & Cold. by J.T. Bowen, Phil.

No. 1.

Plate II

Drawn on Stone by R. Trembly

Maryland. Marmot. Woodchuck. Groundhog

Old & Young.

Drawn from Nature by J.J. Audubon F.R.S. F.L.S.

Printed by Nagel & Weingaertner N.Y.

No. 27. Plate CXXXIV.

Drawn from Nature by J.W.Audubon. On stone by W.E.Hitchcock. Lith. Printed & Col. by J.T.Bowen, Philada

Yellow-bellied Marmot.

N°. 16

Plate LXXX

Leconte's Pine Mouse

Drawn from Nature by J. J. Audubon, F.R.S. F.L.S.

Lith. Printed & Col^{d} by J. T. Bowen, Phil.

N°26

Plate CXXIX

On Stone by Wm E [illegible]

Drawn from Nature by J.W. Audubon

Northern Meadow Mouse

Lith. Printed & Col^d by J.T. Bowen, Phil.

N° 30 Plate CXLVII

Fig. 1 Fig. 2 Fig. 3

On Stone by Wm. E. Hitchcock

Fig. 1 American Souslik. Fig. 2 Oregon Meadow Mouse. Fig. 3 Texan Meadow Mouse

Drawn from Nature by J. W. Audubon

Lith. Printed & Cold. by J. T. Bowen, Phil.

N°27.

Plate CXXXV.

Drawn from Nature by J W Audubon

On stone by W.E. Hitchcock

Richardson's Meadow Mouse

Lith.d Printed & Col.d by J T Bowen, Philad:

No. 29

Plate CXLIV

On Stone by Wm. E Hitchcock

Fig 1. Townsend's Arvicola. Fig 2 Sharp-nosed Arvicola. Fig 3. Bank Rat

Drawn from Nature by J.W. Audubon

Lith. Printed & Cold. by J.T. Bowen, Phil

No. 9. Plate XLV.

Drawn on Stone by Wm E. Hitchcock.

Drawn from Nature by J.J. Audubon, F.R.S. F.S.S.

Lith. Printed & Col.d by J.T. Bowen, Philada.

No. 23.

Plate CXV.

On Stone by W. E. Hitchcock

Drawn from Nature by J. W. Audubon

Yellow-Cheeked Meadow Mouse.

Lith.d Printed & Col.d by J. T. Bowen, Philada.

No 20 Plate XCVIII

On Stone by Wm E Hitchcock

Ring-Tailed Bassaris.

Drawn from Nature by J W Audubon

Lith Printed & Col^d by J T Bowen, Phil

No. 12.

Plate LVI

On Stone by Wm. E. Hitchcock.

American Bison or Buffalo.

Drawn from Nature by J. J. Audubon, F.R.S. F.L.S.

Lith. Printed & Cold. by J. T. Bowen, Phil.

No. 12

Plate LVII

On Stone by Wm E. Hitchcock

Drawn from Nature by J.J. Audubon, F.R.S.F.L.S.

American Bison or Buffalo

Printed & Col^{d} by J.T. Bowen, Philad^{a}

No. 14

Plate LXVII

On Stone by W.E. Hitchcock

Black American Wolf

Drawn from Nature by J. W. Audubon

Lith. Printed & Col^{d} by J.T. Bowen, Phil.

Plate CXIII.

No. 23.

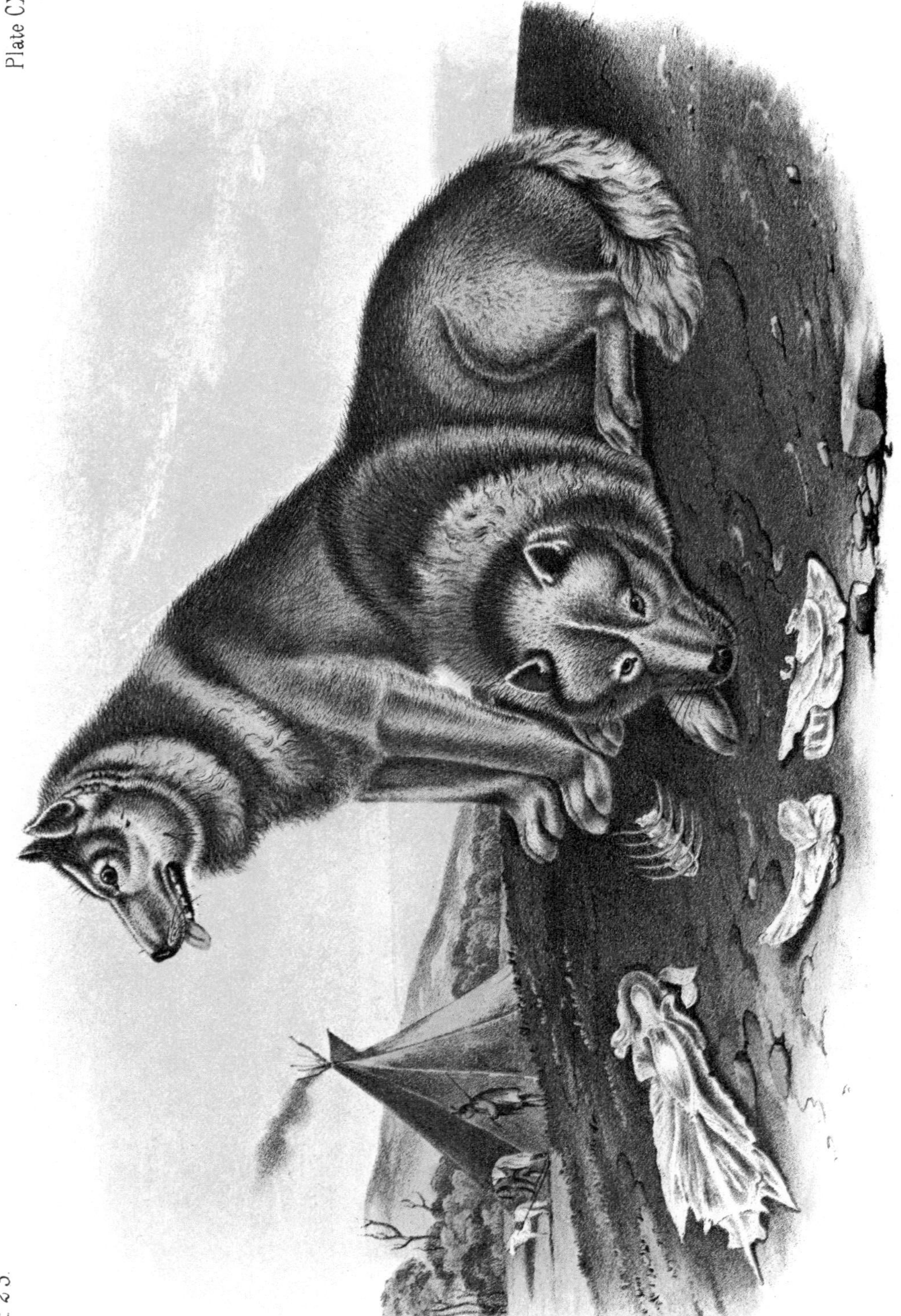

Esquimaux Dog.

Drawn from Nature by J.W Audubon

Drawn on Stone by Wm. E. Hitchcock

Lith. Printed & Col'd by J.T. Bowen, Phil.

No. 27.

Plate CXXXII

On stone by W.E. Hitchcock.

Drawn from Nature by J.W. Audubon

Hare-Indian Dog.

Lith Printed & Col^d by J.T. Bowen, Philad^a

No. 15. Plate LXXI.

On Stone by Wm. E. Hitchcock

Prairie Wolf.

Drawn from Nature by J. W. Audubon

Lith. Printed & Cold. by J. T. Bowen, Philad.

No. 17. Plate LXXXII.

On stone by W. E. Hitchcock

Drawn from Nature by J. W. Audubon.

Red Texan Wolf.

Lith.d Printed & Col.d by J. T. Bowen, Philad.a

N°. 15

Plate LXXII

On Stone by W^m. E. Hitchcock

White American Wolf

Drawn from Nature by J. W. Audubon

Lith. Printed & Col^d. by J. T. Bowen, Phil.

No. 26 Plate CXXVIII

Drawn from Nature by J W Audubon On Stone by Wm E. Hitchcock Lith Printed & Col'd by J T Bowen, Phila.

Rocky Mountain Goat.

N° 10. Plate XLVI

On Stone by W. E. Hitchcock

American Beaver.

Drawn from Nature by J.J. Audubon, F.R.S.F.L.S

Lith. Printed & Col[d] by J.T. Bowen, Philada.

N° 16

Plate LXXVIII

On Stone by Wm E. Hitchcock

Black-tailed Deer

Drawn from Nature by J. W. Audubon

Lith. Printed & Col^d^ by J. T. Bowen, Phil

N° 22.

Plate CVI.

On Stone by W. E. Hitchcock.

Drawn from Nature by J. W. Audubon.

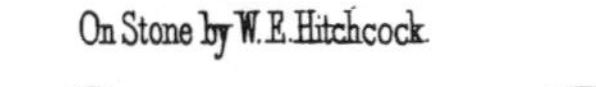

Columbian Black-Tailed Deer.

Lith.d Printed & Col.d by J. T. Bowen, Philad.a

N°. 17.

Plate LXXXI

On Stone by Wm. E. Hitchcock

Drawn from Nature by J. W. Audubon

Common American Deer.

Lith. Printed & Col.d by J. T. Bowen, Phil.

No 28

Plate CXXXVI

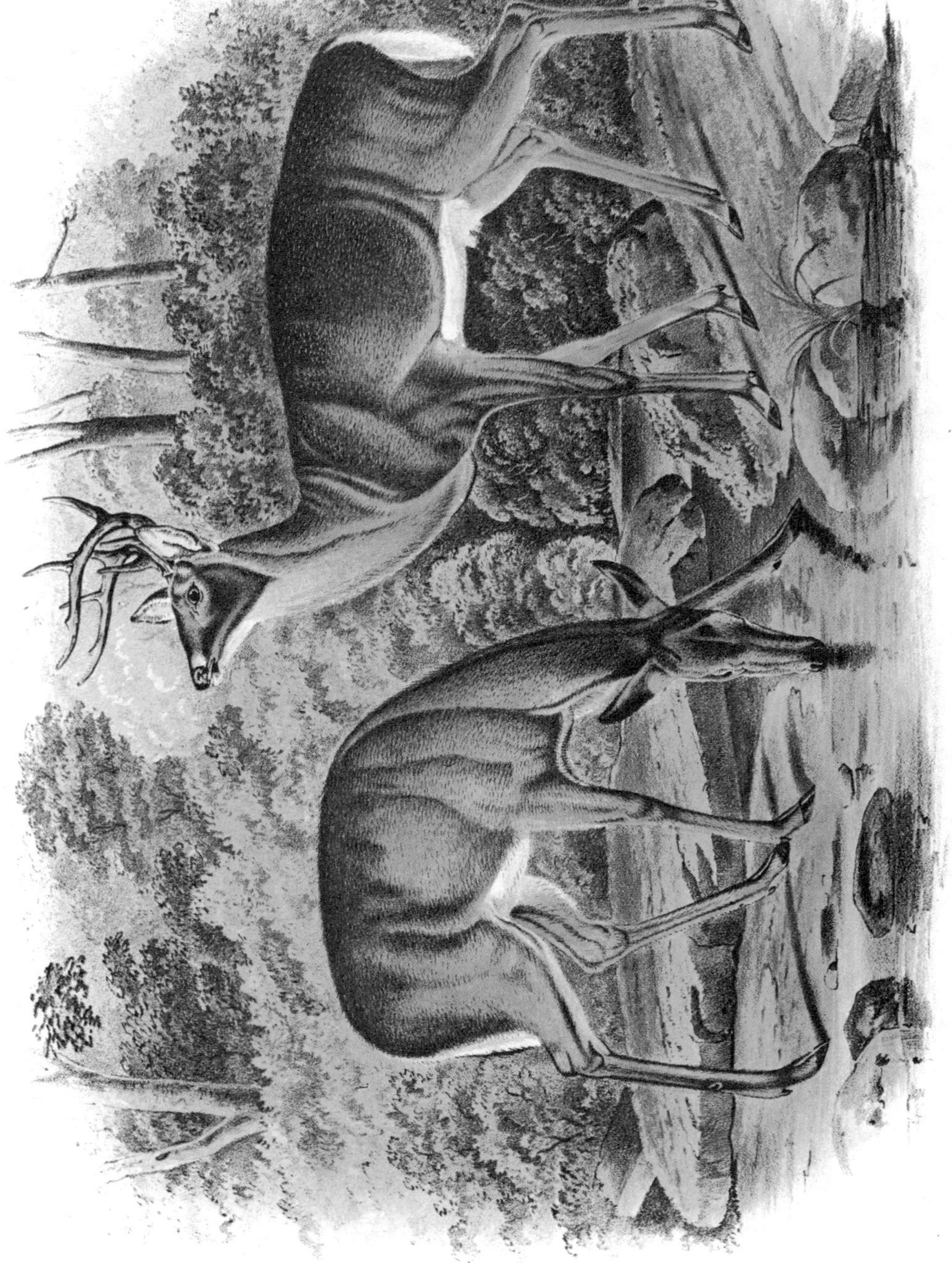

Drawn from Nature by J. W. Audubon

On Stone by Wm E. Hitchcock

Lith Printed & Col'd by J T Bowen, Phil

Common or Virginian Deer.

No. 24. Plate CXVIII

On Stone by W.E. Hitchcock.

Drawn from Nature by J. W. Audubon. *Long-tailed Deer.* Lith.[d] Printed & Col.[d] by J. T. Bowen, Philad.[a]

No. 16. Plate LXXVI

On Stone by W. E. Hitchcock

Drawn from Nature by J. W. Audubon.

Moose Deer

Lith.d Printed & Col.d by J. T. Bowen, Philad.a

N° 14

Plate LXIX

On Stone by W. E. Hitchcock

Drawn from Nature by J. J. Audubon F.R.S.F.L.S.

Common Star-Nose Mole.

N°. 30

Plate CXLVI

On Stone by W^{m}. E. Hitchcock

Drawn from Nature by J. W. Audubon

Nine-banded Armadillo

Lith. Printed & Col^{d}. by J. T. Bowen, Phil

N° 14

Plate LXVI

On Stone by Wm E. Hitchcock

Virginian Opossum.

Drawn from Nature by J. J. Audubon, F.R.S.F.L.S.

Lith. Printed & Col^d^ by J. T. Bowen, Phil.

On Stone by Wm E. Hitchcock

Drawn from Nature by J W Audubon

Pouched Jerboa Mouse

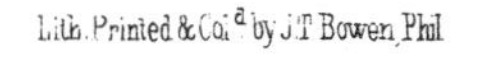
Lith. Printed & Col.d by J.T. Bowen, Phil.

N°. 7

Plate XXXI

Drawn on Stone by R Trembly.

Collared Peccary.

Drawn from Nature by J.J. Audubon F.R.S, F.L.S.

Printed by Nagel & Weingærtner N.Y.

Plate LXII

On Stone by W.E. Hitchcock

Drawn from Nature by J.J. Audubon, F.R.S.F.L.S.

American Elk.– Wapiti Deer.

Lith. Printed & Col.d by J. T. Bowen, Phil.

N°28.

Plate CXXXVII.

Drawn from Nature by J. W. Audubon.

Sea Otter

Lith. Printed & Col.d by J. T. Bowen, Philad.a

N° 20.
Plate XCVII
The Cougar
Drawn from Nature by J. W. Audubon
Lith Printed & Col^d by J. T. Bower, Phil
Female & Young.

No 20 Plate XCVI

Drawn on Stone by Wm E. Hitchcock

Drawn from Nature by J.W. Audubon

The Cougar.

Male.

Lith Printed & Col^d by J.T. Bowen, Phil.

No. 21 Plate CI.

On Stone by W.E. Hitchcock

Drawn from Nature by J.W. Audubon. Lith.d Printed & Col.d by J.T. Bowen, Phila.d

The Jaguar.

N° 18

Plate LXXXVI

On Stone by Wm E. Hitchcock

Drawn from Nature by J W Audubon

Ocelot or Leopard-Cat.

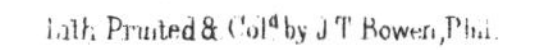

Lith. Printed & Col'd by J T Bowen, Phil.

N°. 3

Plate XIII

Drawn on Stone by Wm. E. Hitchcock

Drawn from Nature by J.J.Audubon, F.R.S.F.L.S

Lith. Printed & Cold. by J.T. Bowen, Phil

Musk Rat. _ Musquash.

Old & Young.

N° 24

Plate CIX

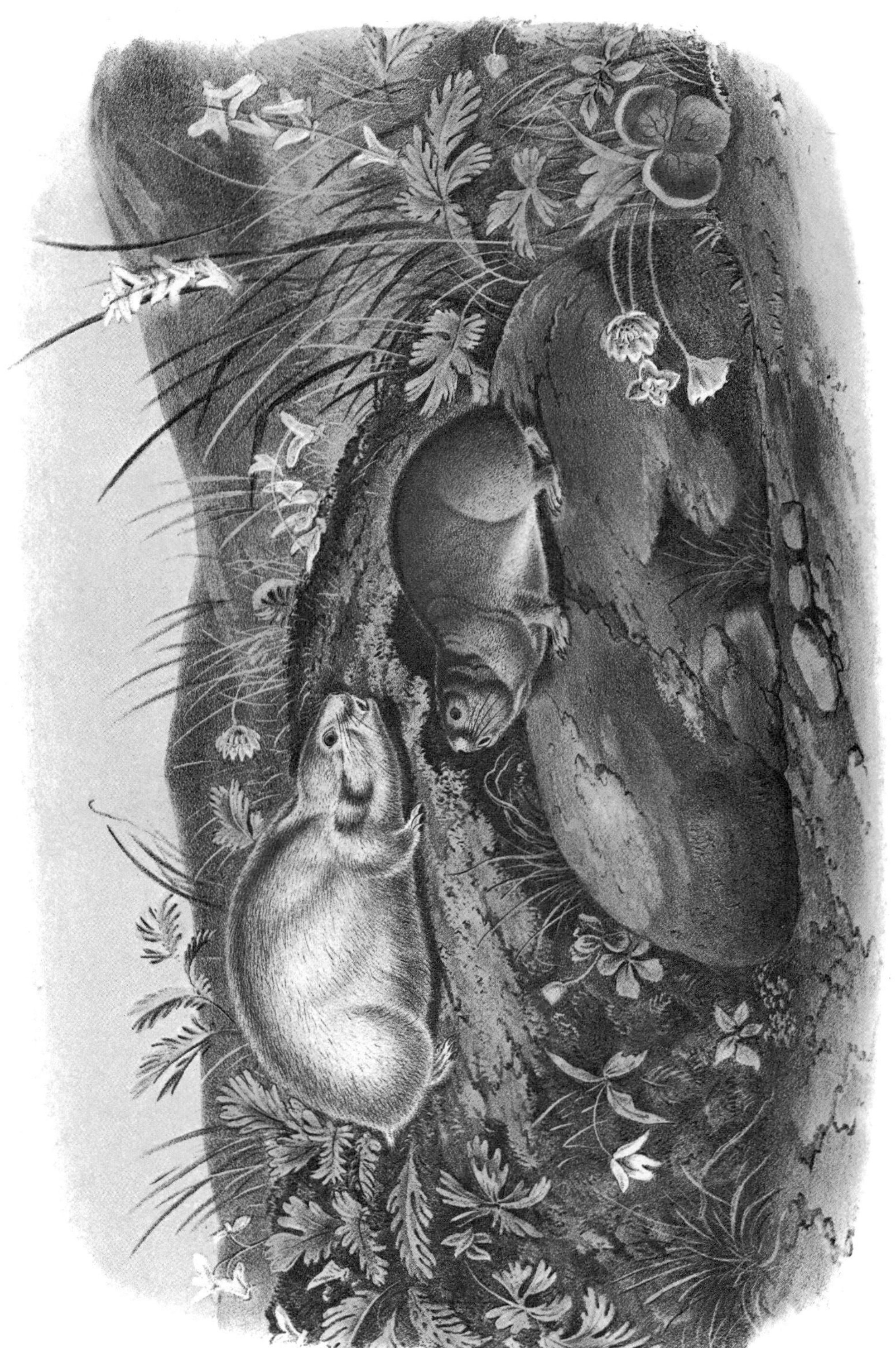

Drawn from Nature by J.W. Audubon

Drawn on Stone by Wm E. Hitchcock

Lith Printed & Col^d^ by J.T. Bowen, Phil

Hudson's Bay Lemming

No 24 Plate CXX

2.3

Drawn on Stone by Wm E Hitchcock

Drawn from Nature by J. W. Audubon — Lith. Printed & Col.d by J. T. Bowen, Phil.

Fig. 1 Tawny Lemming — Figs 2 & 3 Back's Lemming

N° 6. Plate XXVI.

Drawn on stone by R. Trembly

Wolverine.

Drawn from Nature by J. J. Audubon, F.R.S.F.L.S.

Printed & Col^d by J. T. Bowen, Philad^a

No. 8. Plate XXXVI.

Canada Porcupine.

Drawn from Nature by J.J. Audubon F.R.S.F.L.S. Lith.d, Printed & Col.d by J.T. Bowen, Philad.a

N°. 17

Plate LXXXIII

On Stone by Wm. E. Hitchcock

Little Chief Hare.

Drawn from Nature by J. J. Audubon, F.R.S.F.L.S.

Lith. Printed & Col^{d} by J. T. Bowen, Phil.

No. 22

Plate CVIII

On Stone by W.E. Hitchcock

Drawn from Nature by J.W. Audubon

Bachman's Hare

Lith.d Printed & Col.d by J.T. Bowen Philad.a

N°. 13

Plate LXIII

On Stone by W. E. Hitchcock

Drawn from Nature by J. J. Audubon, F.R.S.F.L.S

Black-tailed Hare.

Lith. Printed & Col.d by J. T. Bowen, Philad.a

N°. 23

Plate CXII.

Drawn on stone by W.E. Hitchcock

Drawn from Nature by J. W. Audubon.

Californian Hare.

Lith^{d} Printed & Col^{d} by J. T. Bowen, Philad^{a}

No. 5

Plate XXII

Drawn on Stone by R. Trembly.

Grey Rabbit.

Old & Young.

Drawn from Nature by J J Audubon, F.R.S., F.L.S.

Printed by Nagel & Weingærtner, N.Y.

N°. 4 Plate XVIII

Drawn on Stone by R Trembly

Marsh Hare.

Drawn from Nature by J.J.Audubon F.R.S.F.L.S. Printed by Nagel & Weingærtner N.Y.

No. 3. Plate XI

Northern Hare — (Old & Young)

Summer pelage.

Drawn from Nature by J. J. Audubon F.R.S.F.L.S.

Drawn on Stone by R. Trembly.

Printed by Nagel & Weingaertner N.Y.

Plate XII

N°3.

Northern Hare

Winter pelage.

Drawn from Nature by J. J. Audubon F.R.S. F.L.S.

Drawn on Stone by R. Trembly.

Printed by Nagel & Weingartner N.Y.

Colored by J. Lawrence

N° 19

Plate XCIV

On Stone by Wm E. Hitchcock

Drawn from Nature by J.W. Audubon

Nuttall's Hare.

Lith. Printed & Col^d by J.T. Bowen, Phil.

N° 7. Plate XXXII.

Drawn on stone by R. Trembly

Drawn from Nature by J. J. Audubon, F.R.S.F.L.S.

Polar Hare.

Printed & Col^{d}. by J. T. Bowen, Philad^{a}.

N° 8. Plate XXXVII.

Drawn on Stone by R. Trembly

Swamp Hare

Male.

Drawn from Nature by J.J. Audubon, F.R.S. F.L.S.

Lith Printed & Col.d by J.T. Bowen, Phil.

No. 27. Plate CXXXIII.

Drawn from Nature by J. W. Audubon. On stone by W. E. Hitchcock. Lith. Printed & Col.d by J. T. Bowen, Philad.a

Texian Hare.

No. I. Plate III.

Drawn on Stone by R. Trembly

Townsend's Rocky Mountain Hare

Drawn from Nature by J.J. Audubon F.R.S, F.L.S

Male & Female

Printed by Nagel & Weingærtner N.Y.

No. 18 Plate LXXXVIII.

On Stone by W. E. Hitchcock.

Worm-wood Hare.

Drawn from Nature by J. J. Audubon, F.R.S. F.L.S. Lith.d Printed & Col.d by J. T. Bowen, Philad.a

N°11

Plate LI

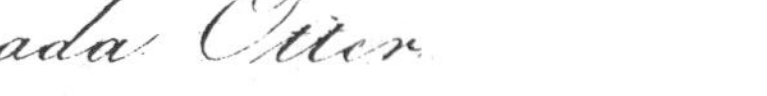

Drawn from Nature by J. J. Audubon F.R.S. F.L.S.

Canada Otter

Lith Printed & Col.d by J. T. Bowen, Philad.a

N°. 25

Plate CXXII

On Stone by W^m E Hitchcock

Drawn from Nature by J.W Audubon

No. 4

Plate XVI

Drawn on Stone by R. Trembly

Canada Lynx.

Male

Drawn from Nature by J.J. Audubon F.R.S.F.L.S.

Printed by Nagel & Weingærtner N.Y.

No. 1. Plate I.

Drawn on Stone by R. Trembly

Common American Wild-cat.

Male.

Drawn from Nature by J. J. Audubon F.R.S. F.L.S.

Printed by Nagel & Weingaertner N.Y.

No. 19

Plate XCII

On Stone by Wm. E. Hitchcock

Drawn from Nature by J. W. Audubon

Texan Lynx.

Lith. Printed & Col^d by J. T. Bowen, Phil.

N°. 10

Plate XLVII

Drawn from Nature by J.J. Audubon, F.R.S.F.L.S

American Badger

Lith. Printed & Col.d by J.T. Bowen, Philada

Common American Skunk.

Drawn from Nature by J. J. Audubon, F.R.S.F.L.S. Lith Printed & Colᵈ by J. T. Bowen, Philadᵃ

N°. 21 Plate CII.

On Stone by W.E. Hitchcock.

Large-Tailed Skunk.

Drawn from Nature by J.W. Audubon. Lith⁴ Printed & Col⁴ by J.T. Bowen, Philad^a.

No. 11

Plate LIII

Drawn from Nature by J.J. Audubon, F.R.S.F.L.S.

On Stone by Wm E. Hitchcock

Lith. Printed & Col.d by J.T. Bowen, Phil.

Texan Skunk.

No. 17.

Plate LXXXV

On Stone by Wm. E. Hitchcock

Drawn from Nature by J. J. Audubon F.R.S F.L.S

Jumping Mouse.

Lith. Printed & Cold. by J. T. Bowen Phil.

N° 8

Plate XL

Drawn on Stone by Wm. E. Hitchcock

White Footed Mouse.

Drawn from Nature by J.J. Audubon F.R.S. F.L.S.

Lith. Printed & Cold. by J.T. Bowen, Philada.

N°. 5

Plate XXIII

Drawn on Stone by R Trembly.

Black Rat

Old & Young.

Drawn from Nature by J.J.Audubon, F.R.S.F.L.S.

Printed by Nagel & Weingærtner, N.Y.

N°. 11

Plate LIV

On Stone by Wm. E. Hitchcock.

Drawn from Nature by J. J. Audubon, F.R.S.F.L.S

Brown or Norway Rat

Lith. Printed & Col^{d} by J. T. Bowen, Phil.

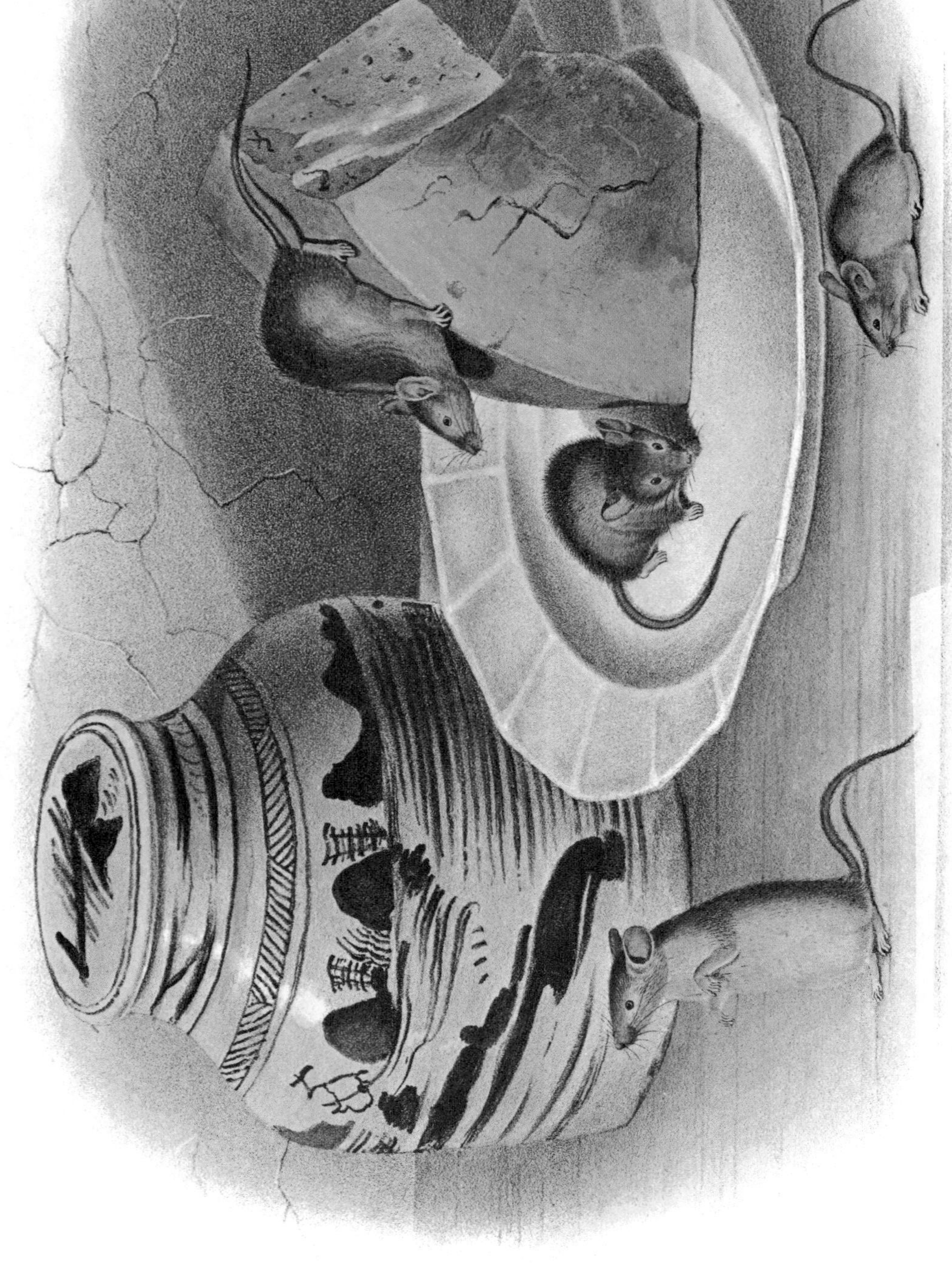

Plate XC
No 18
Drawn from Nature by J.W. Audubon
On Stone by Wm E. Hitchcock
Common Mouse.
Lith Printed & Cold by J.T. Bowen, Phil

Plate LXV.

N° 13

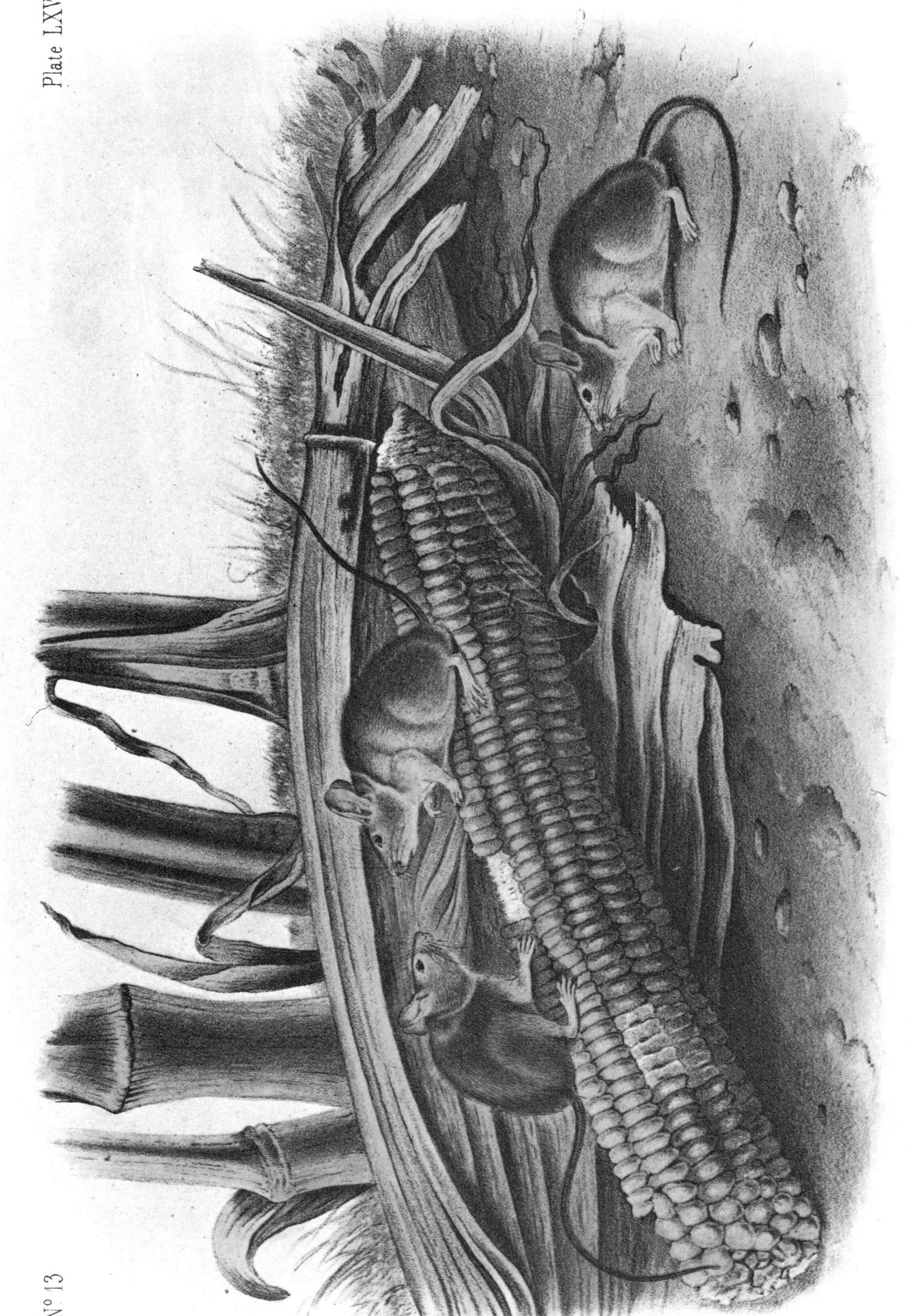

Drawn from Nature by J.J. Audubon, F.R.S.F.L.S.

On Stone by W E Hitchcock

Little Harvest Mouse.

N°. 20

Plate C.

On Stone by W.E.Hitchcock.

Drawn from Nature by J.W.Audubon.

Lith^d. Printed & Col^d. by J.T.Bowen, Philad^a.

Missouri Mouse.

N°19

Plate XCV

On Stone by Wm E. Hitchcock

Drawn from Nature by J.W. Audubon

Orange Colored Mouse

Lith. Printed & Col^d. by J.T. Bowen, Phil.

N°9.

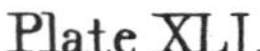

Plate XLI.

Drawn on Stone by W. E. Hitchcock

Pennants Marten or Fisher.

Drawn from Nature by J. J. Audubon, F.R.S. F.L.S.

Lith.^d Printed & Col.^d by J. T. Bowen, Philad.^a

N° 28

Plate CXXXVIII

On Stone by W E Hitchcock

Drawn from Nature by J W Audubon

Pine Marten

Lith Printed & Col[d] by J T Bowen, Phil

N° 1 Plate IV

Drawn on Stone by Wm. E. Hitchcock

Florida Rat.

Male, Female & Young of different ages

Drawn from Nature by J. J. Audubon, F.R.S.F.L.S Lith Printed & Col.d by J. T. Bowen, Phil

No. 6

Plate XXIX

Drawn on Stone by R. Trembly

Drawn from Nature by J.J. Audubon F.R.S.F.L.S.

Printed by Nagel & Weingærtner N.Y.

Plate CXI.

N.° 23

Drawn from Nature by J.W.Audubon.

Drawn on Stone by W.m E. Hitchcock

Lith. Printed & Col.d by J.T. Bowen, Phil.

Musk Ox.

No. 15

Plate LXXIII

On Stone by Wm. E. Hitchcock

Drawn from Nature by J. W. Audubon

Lith. Printed & Cold. by J. T. Bowen, Phil.

Rocky Mountain Sheep.

No. 31. Plate CLV

On Stone by Wm. E. Hitchcock

Drawn from Nature by J. W. Audubon

Crab-eating Raccoon

Lith. Printed & Col.d by J. T. Bowen, Phil.

On Stone by W. H. Hitchcock

Raccoon.

Drawn from Nature by J. W. Audubon

Lith. Printed & Col^{d} by J. T. Bowen, Phil

N° 29

Plate CXLII.

On Stone by Wm E. Hitchcock

Drawn from Nature by J. W. Audubon

Lith. Printed & Col^d by J. T. Bowen, Phil^a

The Camas Rat

No. 9. Plate XLIV

Canada Pouched Rat.

Drawn from Nature by J. J. Audubon F.R.S. F.L.S.

Lith. Printed & Col[d] by J. T. Bowen, Philada.

No. 21 Plate CV.

On Stone by W.E. Hitchcock

Drawn from Nature by J.W. Audubon. Lith.d Printed & Col.d by J.T. Bowen, Philada.

Columbia Pouched Rat.

No. 22. Plate CX.

On Stone by W.E. Hitchcock.

Drawn from Nature by J. W. Audubon.

Mole-Shaped Pouched Rat.

Lith^d. Printed & Col^d. by J. T. Bowen, Philad^a.

N° 30

Plate CL.

On Stone by W^m. E Hitchcock

Fig. 1. Southern Pouched Rat. Fig. 2. Dekay's Shrew. Fig. 3. Long-Nosed Shrew. Fig. 4 Silvery Shrew Mole.

Drawn from Nature by J.W. Audubon

Lith. Printed & Col^d. by J.T. Bowen, Phil

No. 6 Plate XXVIII

Drawn on Stone by R. Trembly

Common Flying Squirrel

1, 2 Males, 3, 4 Females, 5 Young

Drawn from Nature by J.J. Audubon F.R.S. F.L.S.

Printed by Nagel & Weingærtner N.Y.

N°. 3 Plate XV

Drawn on Stone by Wm. E. Hitchcock

Oregon Flying Squirrel.

Drawn from Nature by J. J. Audubon, F.R.S.F.L.S.

Lith. Printed & Col.d by J. T. Bowen, Phil.

Fig 1. Severn River Flying Squirrel

Fig 2 Rocky Mountain Flying Squirrel

N°19

Plate XCIII

On Stone by Wm E. Hitchcock

Drawn from Nature by J.W. Audubon

Black Footed Ferrett

Lith Printed & Col[d] by J.T. Bowen, Phil

N°12

Plate LX

On Stone by Wm E. Hitchcock

Drawn from Nature by J. J. Audubon. F.R.S. F.L.S.

Bridled Weasel.

Lith. Printed & Col^{d} by J. T. Bowen, Philad^{a}

N°. 13

Plate LXIV

On Stone by W.H. Hitchcock

Little American Brown Weasel.

Drawn from Nature by J.W. Audubon

Lith. Printed & Col^{d} by J.T. Bowen, Phil.

No. 28. Plate CXL

Drawn from Nature by J. W. Audubon. On stone by W.E.Hitchcock. Lith.d Printed & Col.d by J.T. Bowen. Philad.a

Little Nimble Weasel.

No. 7. Plate XXXIII.

Drawn on stone by R. Trembly

Mink.

Male & Female

Drawn from Nature by J. J. Audubon, F.R.S. F.L.S.

Printed & Col.d by J. T. Bowen, Philad.a

No 25 Plate CXXIV

Mountain Brook Mink.

Drawn from Nature by J.W. Audubon On Stone by Wm E. Hitchcock Lith. Printed & Col'd by J.T. Bowen, Phil.

No. 30

Plate CXLVIII

On Stone by Wm E. Hitchcock

Drawn from Nature by J.W. Audubon

Tawny Weasel.

Lith. Printed & Col.d by J.T. Bowen, Phil.

No. 12. Plate LIX.

White Weasel, Stoat.

Drawn from Nature by J. J. Audubon, F.R.S.F.L.S.

Lith.d Printed & Col.d by J. T. Bowen, Philad.a

N°26

Plate CXXVI

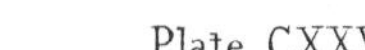

On Stone by Wm E. Hitchcock

Caribou or American Rein-Deer

Drawn from Nature by J. W. Audubon

Lith. Printed & Col^{d} by J. T. Bowen, Phil.

No. 15 Plate LXXIV

On Stone by W. E. Hitchcock

Drawn from Nature by J. J. Audubon, F.R.S.F.L.S.

Brewer's Shrew Mole

Lith. Printed & Col.d by J. T. Bowen, Phila.

N° 2

Plate X

Drawn on Stone by W.E. Hitchcock.

Drawn from Nature by J.J. Audubon F.R.S. F.L.S.

Lith^d Printed & Col^d by J. T. Bowen, Philad^a

Common American Shrew Mole.

Male & Female.

No. 29

Plate CXLV

On Stone by Wm. E. Hitchcock

Drawn from Nature by J. W. Audubon

Townsend's Shrew Mole

Lith. Printed & Col.d by J. T. Bowen, Phil.

N°7 Plate XXXIV

Black Squirrel.

Drawn from Nature by J.J. Audubon, F.R.S F.L.S. Lith.ᵈ Printed & Col.ᵈ by J.T. Bowen, Philad.ᵃ

No. 2 Plate VII

Drawn on Stone by R. Trembly.

Carolina Grey Squirrel.

Male & Female.

Drawn from Nature by J. J. Audubon F.R.S.F.L.S. Printed by Nagel & Weingærtner, N.Y.

No. 4 Plate XVII

Cat Squirrel

Drawn from Nature by J. J. Audubon FRS FLS

Drawn on Stone by R. Trembly

Printed by Nagel & Weingærtner NY

Colored by J. Lawrence

N.° 31

Plate CLIII

Fig. 2

Fig. 1

Fig 1 Col. Abert's Squirrel. – Fig. 2. California Grey Squirrel

Drawn from Nature by J.W. Audubon

Lith Printed & Col.d by J.T. Bowen, Phil

N°. 21 Plate CIV

On Stone by Wm. E. Hitchcock.

Collies Squirrel

Drawn from Nature by J. W. Audubon

Lith. Printed & Col.d by J. T. Bowen, Ph.

No. 5 Plate XXV

Drawn on Stone by R. Trembly

Downy Squirrel.

Drawn from Nature by J.J. Audubon F.R.S. F.L.S. Printed by Nagel & Weingaertner N.Y.

No. 10. Plate XLVIII

On Stone by Wm. H. Hitchcock

Douglass Squirrel.

Drawn from Nature by J.J.Audubon F.R.S.F.L.S. Lith. Printed & Cold. by J.T.Bowen, Phila.

No. 24.

Plate CXVII

On Stone by W.E. Hitchcock.

Dusky Squirrel.

Drawn from Nature by J.W. Audubon.

Lith.d Printed & Col.d by J.T. Bowen, Philad.a

N°30 Plate CXLIX

On Stone by Wm E Hitchcock

Fig. 1 Fremont's Squirrel.— Fig. 2 Sooty Squirrel.

Drawn from Nature by J. W. Audubon

Lith Printed & Col'd by J. T. Bowen, Phil

N° 11 Plate LXVIII

On Stone by [illegible]

Fox Squirrel.

Drawn from Nature by J.J. Audubon, F.R.S.F.L.S. Lith Printed & Col[d] by J.T. Bowen, Phil.

N°9. Plate XLIII.

Drawn on Stone by W.E. Hitchcock.

Hare Squirrel.

Hudson's Bay Squirrel - Chickaree - Red Squirrel.

Drawn from Nature by J. J. Audubon F.R.S., F.L.S. Printed by Nagel & Weingærtner N.Y.

Drawn on Stone by R. Trembly. Colored by J. Lawrence

N° 6. Plate XXVII.

Drawn on stone by R. Trembly

Long Haired Squirrel.

Drawn from Nature by J. J. Audubon, F.R.S. F.L.S. Printed & Col.d by J. T. Bowen, Philad

N° 7 Plate XXXV

On Stone by Wm. E. Hitchcock

Migratory Squirrel.

Drawn from Nature by J. J. Audubon, F.R.S.F.L.S. Lith. Printed & Col.d by J. T. Bowen, Phil

N° 12. Plate LVIII.

On Stone by W.E. Hitchcock

Orange-bellied Squirrel.

Drawn from Nature by J. J. Audubon, F.R.S. F.L.S. Lith.d Printed & Col.d by J. T. Bowen, Philad.a

N.º 8. Plate XXXVIII.

Red-Bellied Squirrel.

Drawn from Nature by J. J. Audubon, F.R.S. F.L.S. Lith.d Printed & Col.d by J. T. Bowen, Philad.a

On Stone by W. E. Hitchcock

Red-tailed Squirrel.

Drawn from Nature by J. J. Audubon, F.R.S.F.L.S

Lith. Printed & Col.d by J. T. Bowen, Philada

N°. 1. Plate V

Drawn on Stone by W^m. E. Hitchcock

Richardson's Columbian Squirrel

Drawn from Nature by J.J. Audubon, F.R.S.F.L.S.

Lith. Printed & Col^d. by J.T. Bowen, Phil

N°18. Plate LXXXIX

Drawn from Nature by J J Audubon, F.R.S F.L.S.

On Stone by Wm. E. Hitchcock

Say's Squirrel

Lith. Printed & Col^{d} by J T Bowen, Philad

Soft haired Squirrel.

Drawn from Nature by J.J. Audubon F.R.S.F.L.S. Printed by Nagel & Weingærtner, N.Y.

Drawn on Stone by R. Trembly.

Fig. 1.

Fig. 2.

Drawn on Stone by Wm. E. Hitchcock.

Fig. 1. Weasel-like Squirrel

Fig. 2. Large Louisiana Black Squirrel.

Drawn from Nature by J.W. Audubon. Lith. Printed & Cold by J.T. Bowen, Phil

N°. 6

Plate XXX

Drawn on Stone by R. Trembly.

Cotton Rat.

Drawn from Nature by J. J. Audubon F.R.S, F.L.S.

Printed by Nagel & Weingærtner NY

Lith. Printed & Col^d by J.T. Bowen, Phil

American Marsh Shrew

No. 15.

Plate LXXV.

On Stone by Wm. E. Hitchcock

Drawn from Nature by J. J. Audubon, F.R.S.F.L.S.

Carolina Shrew

Lith. Printed & Cold. by J. T. Bowen. Phil.

No. 14

Plate LXX.

On Stone by Wm. E. Hitchcock

Say's Least Shrew.

Drawn from Nature by J.J. Audubon, F.R.S.F.L.S.

Lith. Printed & Col.d by J.T. Bowen, Philad

No. 16

Plate LXXIX

On Stone by Wm. E. Hitchcock.

Drawn from Nature by J.J. Audubon, F.R.S.F.L.S

Annulated Marmot Squirrel.

Lith. Printed & Col.d by J.T. Bowen, Phil.

No. 10.

Plate XLIX

Douglasses Spermophile

Drawn from Nature by J.J. Audubon, F.R.S.F.L.S.

Lith.d Printed & Col.d by J.T. Bowen, Philada

Franklin's Marmot Squirrel.

No. 31

Plate CLIV

Drawn from Nature by J.W. Audubon.

On Stone by Wm. E. Hitchcock

Lith. Printed & Col.d by J.T. Bowen, Phil.

Fig. 1 Harris' Marmot-Squirrel Fig. 2 California Meadow-Mouse

No. 8. Plate XXXIX

Drawn on Stone by R. Trembly

Leopard Spermophile.

Drawn from Nature by J. J. Audubon, F.R.S. F.L.S.

Lith. Printed & Col.d by J. T. Bowen, Phil.

Drawn from Nature by J.W. Audubon

On Stone by W.E. Hitchcock

Large-tailed Spermophile

No. 22. Plate. CIX

Drawn on Stone by Wm E. Hitchcock

Drawn from Nature by J.W. Audubon

Mexican Marmot-Squirrel.

Adult male and young

Lith. Printed & Cold by J.T. Bowen, Phil

No. 2

Plate IX

On Stone by Wm. E. Hitchcock

Drawn from Nature by J.J. Audubon, F.R.S.F.L.S

Parry's Marmot Squirrel

Lith. Printed & Col.d by J.T. Bowen, Phil.

N° 20

Plate XCIX.

On Stone by Wm E. Hitchcock

Drawn from Nature by J.J. Audubon, F.R.S.F.L.S.

Prairie Dog.– Prairie Marmot Squirrel.

Lith. Printed & Col.d by J.T. Bowen, Phil.

No. 10. Plate L.

Richardson's Spermophile

Drawn from Nature by J. J. Audubon, F.R.S.F.L.S.

Lith.d Printed & Col.d by J. T. Bowen, Philad.a

No. 23

Plate CXIV.

Drawn on stone by W.E. Hitchcock.

Say's Marmot Squirrel.

Drawn from Nature by J.W. Audubon

Lith. Printed & Col.d by J.T. Bowen, Philad.a

Drawn on Stone by R. Trembly

Chipping Squirrel, Hackee.

Drawn from Nature by J.J. Audubon F.R.S, F.L.S. Printed by Nagel & Weingærtner N.Y.

No. 5 Plate XXIV

Drawn on Stone by R. Trembly

Four striped Ground Squirrel.

Drawn from Nature by J. J. Audubon F.R.S., F.L.S. **1 Male, 2 Female, 3 & 4 Young.** Printed by Nagel & Weingaertner NY

No. 4

Plate XX

Townsend's Ground Squirrel

Drawn from Nature by J J Audubon F.R.S. F.L.S.

Drawn on Stone by R Trembly

Printed by Nagel & Weingærtner N.Y.

Colored by J Lawrence

Plate CXLI
Drawn from Nature by J W Audubon
On Stone by Wm. E. Hitchcock
American Black Bear

No. 26. Plate CXXVII.

On stone by W.E. Hitchcock

Drawn from Nature by J.W. Audubon.

Cinnamon Bear.

Lith[d] Printed & Col[d] by J.T. Bowen, Philad[a]

N°27. Plate CXXXI.

On stone by W.E.Hitchcock

Drawn from Nature by J.W.Audubon

Grizzly Bear.

Lith Printed & Col^{d} by J.T.Bowen, Philad.

Plate XCI
N° 19
On Stone by Wm. E. Hitchcock
Polar Bear.

No. 24

Plate CXVI.

On Stone by W.E. Hitchcock.

Drawn from Nature by J.W. Audubon.

American Black or Silver Fox.

Lith.d Printed & Col.d by J.T. Bowen, Philad.a

N°2.

Plate VI

Drawn from Nature by J.J. Audubon F.R.S. F.L.S.
Drawn on Stone by R. Trembly

American Cross Fox.

Printed by Nagel & Weingærtner N.Y.

N° 18

Plate LXXXVII

Drawn from Nature by J.J.Audubon F.R.S.F.L.S.

On Stone by Wm. E. Hitchcock

Lith. Printed & Cold. by J.T.Bowen, Philad.

American Red-Fox.

No 25

Plate CXXI

Drawn on Stone by Wm E. Hitchcock

Arctic Fox.

Drawn from Nature by J.W. Audubon.

Lith. Printed & Col.d by J.T. Bowen Phil.

No. 5
Plate XXI
Gray Fox.
Male.
Drawn from Nature by J. J. Audubon F.R.S. F.L.S.
Printed by Nagel & Weingærtner N.Y.

No. 31

Plate CLI

On Stone by Wm. E Hitchcock

Drawn from Nature by J.W. Audubon

Lith. Printed & Col[d] by J.T. Bowen, Phil

Jackall Fox.

N° 11.

Plate LII

Drawn on Stone by Wm. E. Hitchcock.

Swift Fox.

Drawn from Nature by J. J. Audubon, F.R.S. F.L.S.

Lith. Printed & Col.d by J. T. Bowen, Philada.

Index

BIRDS—ENGLISH–LATIN

BIRDS—LATIN–ENGLISH

MAMMALS—ENGLISH LATIN

MAMMALS—LATIN-ENGLISH